Reflections
on the First Ten Years

Rev. Mark Ward

Lead Minister

Unitarian Universalist
Congregation of Asheville

Printed in the United States of America

Released by Pisgah Press, LLC
PO Box 1427, Candler, NC 28715
www.pisgahpress.com

Library of Congress Cataloging-in-Publication Data
Reflections on the First Ten Years/Mark Ward

Library of Congress Control Number: 2015931875

ISBN: 978-1942016069
Religion: Meditations
First Printing
April 2015

Introduction

Mark Ward's path and my own crossed more than a quarter of a century ago when I was beginning my ministry at the First Unitarian Society of Madison and he was making his mark as a lay leader at the Unitarian Universalist Church West, in Brookfield, Wisconsin. The two of us did not connect very often—primarily on those occasions when I visited UUCW as a pulpit guest—but over the years we established a rapport upon which a warm and supportive professional relationship eventually was established.

The seeds of that relationship were planted in 2003-2004, when I agreed to supervise Mark's ten-month ministerial internship, the final hurdle to be cleared before his new career could be launched. I had not the slightest hesitation about taking Mark on, knowing full well that he possessed the intellectual acuity and native curiosity, the interpersonal and organizational skills, the commitment and the poise to succeed in the parish ministry. It probably didn't hurt that both his mother and sister were themselves UU ministers so he knew full-well what he was getting into.

And indeed, Mark didn't disappoint. He pursued his internship in Madison with diligence and covered himself with honor. He was the proverbial "quick study" and well before Mark's tenure with us ended, the terms of our relationship had shifted from "intern-supervisor" to "working partners."

Given his impressive skill set and lengthy track record in our UU movement, I was not surprised that the vibrant Unitarian Universalist Congregation of Asheville would tap Mark as their seventh "called" lead minister. It was my honor and privilege to deliver the Charge to the Minister when Mark was duly ordained and installed on February 6, 2005.

It hardly seems possible that ten years have elapsed and that Mark has now served UUCA longer than any of its ministers, save one. And, reading these pulpit addresses, meditations and liturgical pieces, one can see why. This is, I can say with complete honesty, an uplifting and edifying collection that attests to the range of the author's interests and the clarity of his insights.

Moreover, these are not ordinary sermons, but finely crafted essays full of evocative images, engaging metaphors and carefully chosen references. Mark is an analytic thinker and an excellent writer, as one might expect from someone with degrees in philosophy and a solid background in journalism. But few journalists also possess the soul of a poet, as is revealed in these lovely lines: "Bathed in condensation/the landscape draws a deep breath/as if waking to the new day/and we, frowsy with sleep, rise to be with it."

Not all oral presentations translate well onto the printed page, but the sermons in this collection certainly do. They are well structured, the arguments easy to follow and points clearly made. And although the subject matter varies, readers will notice that certain themes are visited and then re-visited, as the author addresses them from various angles.

For instance, "love" figures large in Mark's writing. Having shared his own understanding of that capacious and oft-evoked term, in subsequent essays Mark addresses its prominence in Universalist thought, explores love's place in our most intimate relationships and argues that it should play a much larger role in our daily affairs. "There is inside us this powerful truth, this dazzling wonder, our capacity for transformative love that expresses the best that we are," he writes. "It is what gives us the courage to widen the circle when our fears counsel to keep it closed."

Mark also retains an avid interest in science, an area in which he specialized as a newspaper man. He addresses the ambiguous relationship of science and religion, traces the development of Charles Darwin's thinking and shows how an awareness of certain natural processes can inform our spirituality. In yet another sermon Mark discusses traditional Iroquois teachings and their relevance today as we strive to meet the challenges of resource depletion and climate change.

In those essays directly addressing religion, Mark demonstrates the objectivity and even-handedness of an accomplished journalist. He shows how god language can remain meaningful even to those who no longer subscribe to conventional theism. In another place he raises the possibility that one can be a "spiritual" atheist. And, to those who contend that morality requires a belief in God, Mark offers this rejoinder: "A more reliable indication of moral behavior...is one's ability, as evidenced in one's actions, to see beyond the end of one's nose...recognizing that the interests of others bear on us."

In short, this is a collection well worth lingering over. It is often said that sermons have a relatively short shelf-life because they are directed at a particular audience with its own immediate and parochial concerns. But some sermons wear better than others and can profitably be read and reflected upon years and even decades after their initial airing. This small collection lives up to that promise, and as someone who has himself been writing sermons for nearly four decades I can recommend it to you with confidence.

Michael A. Schuler

DEDICATION

I'm grateful for all who have companioned me on this journey, especially my wife and life's partner, Debbie, and my family by birth and marriage, whose love grounds and centers me. I am grateful for the forbearance, love and support that I have received in these ten years at the Unitarian Universalist Congregation of Asheville. It is my hope that this dance of ministry will have served you and the hope that is our religious movement well, and it is to that hope that this book is dedicated.

Mark Ward

Contents

Part III

Part IV

REFLECTIONS
ON THE FIRST TEN YEARS

PART I

Opening Words

Ten is such a neat, definitive number. In some way, it always seems to signal a beginning and an ending, a commencement and a conclusion. The decade gives us a chunk of time with which to measure our lives: "Oh, that was back in the '60s." "Where were you in the '80s?" It carries some weight.

So, my having concluded ten years as the called lead minister of the Unitarian Universalist Congregation of Asheville seemed a fitting moment to take stock of what has come of my time here. Ministry has many dimensions that are hard to measure or even describe, but there is one moment in my work week that is very public, and it comes with a discipline and a deadline: the Sunday sermon. At least thirty Sundays a year I have prepared and delivered to this congregation words that I hoped would inspire or intrigue, challenge or console, words that spoke to their—to our—need to live with integrity and love, to serve a larger good, to see beyond our comfort and risk seeing ourselves in the oppressed, to breathe together in the company of mystery deeper than we can know.

I cannot know the larger impact of these, what, now 300 sermons. I only know that struggling to give them birth and offer them to a community I have come to love has changed me in the best ways. Just ten years, and so much has changed. My wife, Debbie, and I have lost parents and gained a son-in-law and grandchildren. We have lived with similar losses and gains in the larger church community, all of which together with the tides of our time echo through these sermons and reflections. So, while these words are mine, they are also part of a larger narrative of one gathered people in the first decade of the 21st century.

The thread of these sermons, plus selected newsletter columns and meditations, is roughly though not precisely chronological. I chose them for the breadth of subject matter and in some cases simply because they appealed to me. May you, dear reader, find here something of use.

THIS REFULGENT MOMENT

First candidating sermon
Unitarian Universalist Church of Asheville
April 18, 2004

I date the time of my first awakening to being a part of a church to a bright spring morning—something like this—in the early 1960s. My family had just arrived for Sunday services at the Unitarian Church of Princeton, New Jersey, and as everyone was getting out of the car, I, as usual, had scampered ahead to join some friends playing on the hillside that the church was perched on.

Dashing about and climbing among the bushes as other families gathered and greeted each other, I was aware at some level I couldn't have articulated at the time of being in a safe, welcoming place. I mattered here, and, more than that, we mattered, as individuals and as a gathered assembly. We mattered for who we were, for who were to each other, and for what we were doing. I had no theological context for this at the time. I didn't need one. It was present in the faces before me, in the attention we gave to each other and the joy we took from that.

You might say, as our reading earlier from *The Little Prince* suggests, that we were "taming" each other. The feral natures we each brought into the world were reaching out—testing, then trusting, negotiating that difficult, often twisting path of discovery. But the crucible that made this meeting possible was the church: a church that affirmed and celebrated each of us, where the spirit of discovery underlay every enterprise. On a spring morning all of that seemed to come together in one time and place, a shining awareness of well-being, of broad and deep connections, of durable hope. You might even call it a refulgent moment.

Ever since I sent Linda Bair the blurbs for this week's and next week's services about a month ago, I've been interested to hear what a buzz I apparently stirred up with that word. Cathy Agrella from the Worship Committee said in an e-mail that ever since reading the sermon title she has been reminding everyone to say "refulgent!" So, let's see how you're doing. Can we all say it together?

Refulgent! Very good.

Then your interim minister, Neil Shadle, mentioned in a phone conversation we had about a week ago that early in his tenure with you, he took some ribbing for the prominent use of "refulgent" in a sermon. And so he, and I'm sure some of you, couldn't help but smile to see it in the blurb for my first sermon.

Now, I must admit that there is something about that word that has a hoity-toity feel to it. It doesn't exactly trip off the tongue. Nor is it a word that most of us are likely to use in conversation—or anywhere else for that matter. It's one of those ornate words covered with bric-a-brac and gingerbread that our slimmed down, dot-com culture is happy to let fall by the wayside.

Still, it retains a resonance among us Unitarian Universalists for its appearance at a pivotal moment in our movement. You heard Dick Stennett read the passage earlier: "In this refulgent summer, it has been a luxury to draw the breath of life. The grass grows, the buds burst, the meadow is spotted with fire and gold in the tint of flowers."

The words are those of Ralph Waldo Emerson, and they come at the beginning of what may be the most influential essay he wrote for the future of liberal religion: his address to the graduating class at Harvard Divinity School in July 1838. Emerson was in many ways an odd choice for that honor. Though he himself had been trained at the Divinity School, he had lasted only a couple of years as pastor of Boston's Second Church before deciding to resign the ministry. He found the routine of parish visits and administering communion distasteful. In fact, Emerson was in the process of breaking the last of his ties to the preaching life when the invitation arrived.

But it wasn't Emerson's status as a minister especially that attracted the students' attention. It was his emerging role as spokesman for a new way of expressing and understanding the religious life. In his earlier book, *Nature*, Emerson had argued that religion is to be found not in the dusty tomes of scripture, but in an "original relation to the universe."

Each of us, he said, has a religious sense, a capacity within us to appreciate a deeper connection to our fellows and the universe. He expressed this as seeing spirit in and through everything. And he said we can experience this anywhere: in the woods, on a quiet street, at home before the fire.

Other preachers at the time, including most Unitarians, insisted that religious understanding came from only one place: study of the Christian scriptures. Inspiring walks through the woods were fine, but enthusiasm over them absent Bible study only made for confusion. Emerson turned their arguments on their heads: Bible study was fine, but look first to your own religious insights. What calls to your soul?

It is hard today to convey how odd the beginning of Emerson's Divinity School address must have sounded to his audience. They were, after all, mostly preachers, or preachers-in-training, and the first place a preacher expects to begin is in scripture. That is where you locate the authority for whatever remarks are to follow. But here goes Emerson, waxing poetically about lovely summer days. What's that about? Robert Richardson, Emerson's biographer, points out that however confused the Divinity School audience might have been, the opening sentence of Emerson's address "is not a casual allusion to the weather or a clearing of the throat. It is the central theological point of the talk. Divinity surrounds the living every day."

There is before us a refulgent world, a shining, radiant, resplendent world, that, in the poet Mary Oliver's words, offers itself to our imaginations. It is there that Emerson locates authority, there and in the very human impulse that perceives and appreciates that world. And not only that, that same intuition also guides our moral judgments. We have within us the innate capacity to judge right and wrong, to know the good and abhor the bad. We need to be not so much instructed as provoked to discover it.

In a deft move, Emerson unhitched religion from a single source. Is there wisdom to be found in the Bible? Of course, but don't stop there. Go on to the Mahabarata, the Qur'an and the Tao Te Ching. Go learn from the chants of the Navaho, the circle of the Wicca and the dancing of the Dervishes. Go on to Darwin's *Beagle*, to Einstein's Vienna and to Sagan's telescope. Go on where your questing heart and soul yearn to know. And as we talk, will we use words like God, spirit, or truth, and, if so, what will we mean by them? No doctrinal answer will do. What makes sense to you? And, why? What have you learned, unlearned, been surprised by?

This is the legacy that Emerson left us, and I think it is the spirit that from those earliest years inspired my own affinity to this religious tradition. Through my teen years, the youth group at the Princeton church was a haven during my own tumultuous growing up. It was a place of social support despite my uncertainties, a place that, in Emerson's words, provoked me to discover and grow.

As for many of our youth, though, college carried me away from church. It was a function as much of the self-defining I had to do as, to be honest, my own frank assessment in those years—the early 1970s—that our movement had become distracted with some hurtful and destructive practices. Those of you who were attending our churches at the time will undoubtedly remember. The pain was probably manifested most acutely in the black empowerment controversy, a divisive struggle that essentially derailed our association's emerging hopes to play a significant role in racial justice. But at a less visible level there was just an awful lot of what I'll call "bad behavior" on the part of a surprising range of people that left many feeling damaged and exploited. From the perspective of a college student, I can tell you, it looked like our religious movement had lost its bearings and was floating, adrift.

By the late '70s, though, when I myself was feeling a little adrift, uncertain of my career path and my place in the world, I ended up back at my parents' home in Princeton, and back at the Princeton church. It was in that church that Debbie and I met and, after I had finished journalism training, got married. My first newspaper job was in Charleston, West Virginia, and so out we drove to the hills of Appalachia, terra incognita to both of us. It was in a tiny lay-led fellowship in Charleston that we came to appreciate another of the great gifts of our movement: the embrace of Universalism.

Some of you have probably heard that sweet little poem by Edwin Markham, a Universalist, called "Outwitted."

> He drew a circle that shut me out—
> heretic, rebel, a thing to flout.
> But Love and I had the wit to win:
> We drew a circle that took him in!

Heretic, rebel: that certainly fit how we felt when we moved to Charleston. We found ourselves in a city where Bibles were presented to children upon completion of public elementary school, where the president of the school board went on regular diatribes about the evils of secular humanism and sought to ban books from school that spoke favorably about evolution.

The fifty or so folks gathered in a little fellowship in an out-of-the-way part of town could hardly be blamed for feeling a bit embattled, and yet that was not the spirit of the place. It was, in fact, a warm and welcoming bunch: a harbor at times for transplants like us and refugees from fundamentalism, but also a home for activists and change agents. Markham's circle-widening was a central part of the culture.

"Love and I had the wit to win." From its origins, that has been the genius of Universalism, its central faith statement: The circle-wideners will always win out over the circle-narrowers. Let us stand on the side of love.

"We arrive out of many singular rooms, walking over the branching streets," writes Kenneth Patton. "We come to be assured that brothers and sisters surround us, to restore their images on our eyes. We enlarge our voices in common speaking and singing. We try again that solitude found in the midst of those who with us seek their hidden reckonings. Our eyes reclaim the remembered faces; their voices stir the surrounding air. The warmth of their hands assures us, and the gladness of our spoken names. This is the reason of cities, of homes, of assemblies in the houses of worship."

For all our refulgent moments, we still need a reason to gather. We need to be about our taming. And that begins with love. It begins by opening ourselves to others, risking the outreach that brings us into contact with people and ways of thinking that are different from us. We stumble occasionally. We make mistakes. But we begin again in love.

It was in Charleston that my adult self awakened to this deep possibility of church life, the possibility of what prophets ranging from the Universalist Clarence Skinner to the Rev. Martin Luther King Jr. called "the beloved community." Church, it turned out, could be a place that not only fed my thirst for meaning, for some sense of my place on this earth; it also could be a place that showed me how it might be to live in deep appreciation of others, to practice the ethical life, to honor and celebrate each other's gifts, and to mourn and support each other in our losses.

My years at the Brookfield, Wisconsin, church have in many ways served as a school for learning what that life is about, from worship to RE outings, from meetings of the board to rehearsals of the choir. I'm still learning, and I can tell you that as thrilled as I am with the prospects of being your next minister, there is part of me that is grieving what I know I must leave there. So it is at all partings, but to me the pang I feel is a testament to the power of what church can accomplish.

Now, I must admit that all this talk of living aligned with love has such a happy hearts-and-flowers sound to it. But don't fool yourselves. There's nothing easy about it. "If the one certainty issuffering, and if the only absolute is doubt, from these alone belief must be wrung, or else the bitter poverty found out. Take anguish for a companion and set out."

Those words of May Sarton that Sarah Delcourt read for us earlier speak to the kind of existential awareness that lurks at the edge of any statement of faith. The Buddha taught that suffering is a fundamental part of living. He identified it as the first noble truth. Actually, the English word "suffering" is not quite right. While there are certainly moments in life when we experience pain, the pervasive feeling Buddhists describe is really more one of unease. The image they offer is of grasping: for riches, for power, for fame … for simple affirmation, for some sense that all the time and energy I put in, all the commitments I hew to so conscientiously, will make a difference in the long run.

And attendant to this suffering, inevitably, is doubt. The teachings, the consolations we receive come up short. You say love will prevail. Oh, really? Well, let me give you chapter and verse of caring people crushed under the unforgiving wheel of history, promising lives cut short, love betrayed and besmirched. The papers are filled with it every day: spirited young men and women carted home from Iraq in body bags, casualties of a zealous, unilateralist aggression; a skyrocketing income gap that rewards a shrinking number of the super-wealthy leaving growing numbers of people with poverty wages; the continuing befouling of the earth; the soul-deadening persistence of racism, classism and homophobia. Where's the hope in that?

You can hear it, can't you? Deep anguish. Anguish that the meaning we hope to find is just an illusion, that our lives will just drag by—nasty, brutish and short. It's an anguish that even the most hopeful and committed of us can fall prey to, including those of us engaged in church life.

So far I've conveyed to you some of the joyful, refulgent

moments that I've experienced in the life of our churches—and I've had many—but let me own up: I've had my moments of anguish there, too. It may be something as simple as this person's agenda colliding with that person's irascibility and the other person's stubbornness that sinks a promising project, or just the hurt that comes from thoughtless criticism or dismissal. We are not always easy with each other in this work, and sometimes the energy and hope that we bring to it falls flat.

It can make for tough, dispiriting times. And it can be so easy to pick yourself up and say, "Forget about this. I'm out of here." Easy, yes: but wait, Sarton urges us, don't turn aside. "Take anguish as a companion and set out." Take the disappointments the world has dealt you, the uncertainty that feeds your daily anxiety; take the hurts from the slights you have received and your own grumpy dissatisfaction. All of this leads us back to our own humanity: our vulnerable, confused selves, but also the gifts and courage we possess to act.

Our anguish shows us our limits, the boundaries of our own skill and understanding. We can't fix it, can't resolve it on our own, or by turning to despair, the "bitter poverty" that Sarton warns of. We must make common cause with others in a community that puts hope and circle-widening at its center.

Once we do this, once "we dare to keep anguish companion," as Sarton puts it, "we feel spring in our throats a living song." We refuse to be imprisoned by hate or fear. The energy that once was dissipated in squabbles is redirected to the wall of wrong that confronts us. In our companionship we find cause for joy, for belief that out of the darkness we will see with clearer eyes.

The Universalist way of love is not a passive, placid affair. It engages us at the core of our being, pushes us past our fears and demands our response. "We find it good," as Sarton remarks, "find it belief enough to be anguish alive, creating love."

And so, this story I have been telling you brings us to this time and place, this shining, refulgent moment when our hopes for this church community come together. In this week ahead we will have an opportunity to get to know each other better and talk about what this church might be and about how ministry might help us accomplish those ends. I'm looking forward to our conversations.

For it is here, in this sanctuary of dreams and wisdom and beauty, that we may come to grow, to be healed, to stretch mind and heart; here that we learn to align ourselves with the good and affirm what gives us hope; here that we might learn the wisdom that liberates, the love that consecrates, and the life that maketh all things new.

Meditation
September 2006

We return today to this house of light and hope,
to this community of truth-seeking, love, and justice.

From the fragmented world of our everyday lives we gather in
common search for wholeness and meaning.

We come to be awakened by fresh insight, enduring wisdom,
and the spirit's call,

We come to celebrate the morning, fresh and familiar faces,
and the mercy of life.

Here we open ourselves to all that life brings – the puzzles, the
epiphanies, the laughter and the tears.

Here we gather, that together we might discover and honor that
which is of greatest worth, that we might learn and remember
the duties we owe to one another, to humankind and the earth.

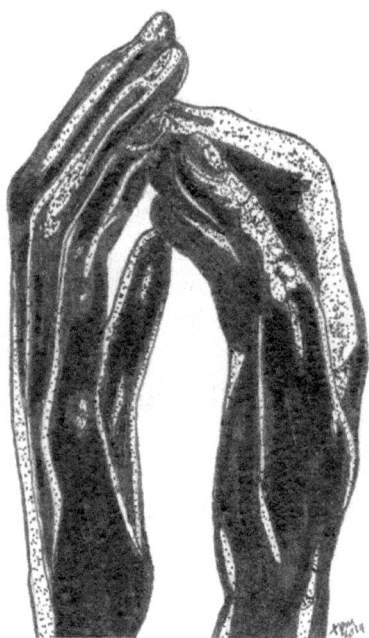

Minister's Musings
January 2014

From time to time you may have seen this sculpture displayed on the table by the pulpit in our sanctuary or on a shelf by the window in my office. It's a reproduction of a piece by Auguste Rodin. I was introduced to it at the Rodin museum on a trip to Paris many years ago. I was taken first by its simple beauty, but then I was even more intrigued when I learned its title: "Le Cathedral." I talked it up a bit at the time of our visit, and later our daughter Anna kindly bought a reproduction for me as a present.

I keep it prominently displayed and look at it often because it seems to me such an apt metaphor for this religious community. It is a representation of two right hands that touch at the wrists and then at the fingers, creating a space between them that is both sheltered and intimate. This, it seems to me, is what we do here. By our commitment to community and our covenant with each other we create holy space where we each might be nurtured to know ourselves as worthy and connected to each other and all things, and encouraged—literally "given heart"—to be agents of freedom, justice and love in the world.

The great cathedrals of Europe were constructed at a time when the goal of religion was something like shock and awe.

The massive structures soaring into the sky communicated eloquently where power lay in those societies and the folly of challenging a prevailing order in which church and state were knit together. Today they are glorious buildings to visit, stunning evidence of human ingenuity, and at the same time a caution of what can happen when religion gets a little too full of itself and confuses power with moral authority.

For me, Rodin's image comes a little closer to what religion exists to do: to give shape and purpose to our aspirations as human beings, to help us see our unity and appreciate the beauty and mystery of this world and this life, and to create a space where we can join in the work required to take us there in a spirit of compassion and joy.

Science and Religion: Can They, Should They, Get Along?

February 11, 2007

It was a summer night some fifteen years ago, and we were gathered together, lying on blankets a little ways from a friend's house out in the country, far from city lights. Our eyes were drinking in the starry sky as one by one we took turns naming constellations we remembered from childhood. Then, suddenly someone called out, "Oh, there's one!" And from the group came a chorus nearly in unison: "Oooo! Ahhh!"

A thin streak of light had just darted across the sky and disappeared, the trace of a chunk of rock left behind in the trail of a comet that had passed by the Earth long ago and had just incinerated before our eyes in the Earth's atmosphere. That explanation for the Perseid meteor shower that we were watching was clear in our heads, yet it was only part of a deeper experience. Taking in the majesty of a sea of stars, the sounds of night around us as we watched meteors streaking with friends gathered near, we sensed a profound connection of earth and sky and life and love.

It is with such experiences in mind that deep in my heart I am both saddened and puzzled by what some call the irreconcilable conflict of science and religion. That's not to say I don't appreciate the past and present-day conflicts between what Stephen Jay Gould called these two "magisteria." What troubles me is the suggestion that these two ways of experiencing the world are essentially incompatible, that somehow we must choose between a religious way of looking at the world and a scientific way of looking at the world.

Curiously, it has been those on the side of science of this question who have been making that argument most strongly of late. I'm thinking particularly of the biologist Richard Dawkins, who in his latest book *The God Delusion* argues that all religion, bar none, is hogwash, even worse, "a very evil" force in the world, and that anything done to eliminate it is a service to humanity.

As his title suggests, Dawkins centers his argument on the belief in God, which he finds not only untenable but delusional. Dawkins also has no use for agnostics, those who profess not to know whether God exists or not, insisting that any credible evidence favors the conclusion that there is no God. In the same way he dismisses Gould's concept of "nonoverlapping magisteria," insisting there is no field of study to which science and logical thought ought to defer to religion.

Nor does he grant any special role for religion in cultivating a moral life, insisting that believers as a rule act no better morally than nonbelievers. Enough of this humble respect that religion demands, Dawkins says. Free humankind of this source of oppression. Be done with it, this vestige of ancient fears that from an evolutionary perspective he equates with the "extravagantly ornate plumage of the bird of paradise":

interesting, perhaps, but something that we as a species would be better off without.

Dawkins's book is certainly entertaining at points, but in the end the problem with it is that the image of religion that he claims to slay is a cardboard cut-out. Sure, any number of horrors over the ages have been perpetrated in the name of religion, and there are some wacky notions peddled in the name of religious faith. To be honest, the same can be said of science. But having said that, what have we proved?

Meanwhile, in dismissing religious people of all stripes as ignorant or deluded, Dawkins ends up merely marginalizing himself. Yes, to be sure evolutionary biologists like himself have been harried by creationists, who envision a 6,000-year-old earth and humans walking the forests in the company of dinosaurs; and by advocates of "intelligent design," who find signs of a creative intelligence in marvels like the human eye. But science itself has done a good job of refuting them, and on the whole they receive little credibility outside the fringe where they reside. A more interesting question is how religion and science will interrelate and learn from each other.

In truth, the conflicts that we experience today are only the latest signs of a seismic shift in human understanding, at least in the West, that has been under way for at least four centuries as science has inexorably replaced religion as the source of our knowledge about the world. Time was that the myths we told of human origins were the province of the church, and in one form or another for centuries the church claimed for itself sole authority to speak on such topics. Bit by bit, though, it has had to give up that claim. The concessions were grudging at best and often fought with every means at the church's disposal, but in time the inexorable power of the scientific method won the day.

And despite the disagreements of a few outliers, most faith

traditions today accept and acknowledge this state of affairs and declare themselves in tune with the picture of the world that science paints. This, of course, leads us to ponder what religion's place in the modern world should be. Dawkins would have us believe that it has none. I disagree.

To answer the question of what role religion might have, I go back to the beginning, the very source of religion itself, which I locate in the human psyche. "A person will worship something, have no doubt about that," wrote Ralph Waldo Emerson. "We may think our tribute is paid in secret in the dark recesses of our hearts, but it will out. That which dominates our imaginations and our thoughts will determine our lives, and our character. Therefore, it behooves us to be careful what we worship, for what we are worshipping we are becoming."

There is within each of us a source of wonder, of meaning, of hope. It guides how we orient and organize our lives. However much we may learn about the world, we are still left with making meaning within it, deciding where we fit in and what our duties are to it and to all with whom we share our journey. This is the work of religion. It is informed by what science teaches, but it is a different discipline from it. It is concerned, as Emerson suggests, with what we worship and why.

And so in that sense I think Stephen Jay Gould was right. As fields of study science and religion are concerned with different things, and that difference is reflected in their origin as words. "Science" comes from the Latin root "scindere," which means to cut, or separate one thing from another, while the world "religion" comes from the Latin root "religare," which means to bind fast. Slicing apart and binding together: no wonder these two can't seem to get along!

And yet, when we take a broader view we see they are part of a larger human journey. Some years ago when I was working as a newspaper science reporter I was asked by my editors to write a story explaining why there seemed to be such a flurry of scientific discovery recently. It was shortly after the cloned sheep Dolly had been born, and scientists were speculating about the evidence of life on a meteorite from Mars. It was a fun story, and the answer to the editor's question was pretty simple: millions of dollars spent over decades on basic research were paying off.

I was especially taken, though, with the response of a biologist I interviewed at the University of Wisconsin. Reflecting on all that science has achieved, he expressed concern over how humankind would cope with the explosion of new knowledge. "If there's a message to come from the Information Age," he said, "it is that we must find a way to convert the information into knowledge, and beyond knowledge, wisdom."

And wisdom, he said, would come from more than just the work of scientists. It would come from the work of artists and philosophers and, yes, religion. Each discipline has its own work to do, but the truth they discover will embrace them all.

I happen to agree with Stephen Jay Gould that moral truth, how we are to live with integrity, is not written in the stars. It is left to us to figure out on our own, and whether we as a species are to prosper or perish depends on the wisdom we are able to glean from our time on Earth.

Religion's role in this is to help us find the connections that can make meaning in our lives. I think of Jennifer Ackerman's observation in the reading you heard earlier that she made watching the tidal communities along Delaware Bay. "The mind," she said, "is peculiarly well equipped to find beauty in the unity among vastly different things." She speaks of the chaos of neurons firing in our brains that makes perception possible being analogous to the chaos of a turbulent flow of water over a bumpy bed of mussels. And from that, she suggests in the words of Wallace Stevens, emerges "the law of ideas, of improvements and seasons of belief."

Our lives, we are learning, are deeply linked with all things, and that alone is a wonder, but beyond that is the question of how, and how that teaches us to be in the world and with each other. After centuries of insisting that our humanity made us exceptional among living things, we are learning that we are at once merely and thankfully a part of it all, a thread in the vast skein of the world.

Science urges us to pull that thread, to find out where it goes and what it's attached to. Religion helps us frame a response to that knowledge: to celebrate it, to integrate it into all that we know and how we live our lives. "At bottom," wrote the philosopher William James, "the whole concern of religion is with the manner of our acceptance of the universe."

What I think he's talking about is not a resigned acceptance but an embrace. It is a matter not of approval, but assent. And as the biologist Ursula Goodenough puts it, "To give assent is to understand, incorporate, and then let go. With the letting go comes that deep sigh we call relief, and relief allows the joy-of-being-alive-at-all to come tumbling forth again."

There is no one way to frame all this. We may use different words, different stories, different metaphors: language that others may or may not consider conventionally religious. Each of us informs the other with the understanding, the insight we glean, and together we build a framework that amounts to our religious response: worship, discussion, meditation, service.

My hope is that our religious life will open us deeply to each other and to every part of the world around us. And in that life we will count every avenue of human endeavor a contributor to the insight, the wisdom we hope to achieve. Doing this will also free us to appreciate every moment we are given. When we stare at the night sky, we will be able to pick out the sky pictures that our ancestors described as they struggled to make sense of the world as well as the red giants, globular clusters and other such denizens with which contemporary astronomy has populated the heavens. We will be able to look at it all and see not what the astronomer Carl Sagan called "a demon-haunted world," but a universe of compelling beauty. We will understand how, in Sagan's words, "science is not only compatible with spirituality; it is a profound source of spirituality."

"When we recognize our place in an immensity of light-years and in the passage of ages, when we grasp the intricacy, beauty and subtlety of life," he wrote, "then that soaring feeling, that sense of elation and humility combined, is surely spiritual."

Now I walk in beauty, the Navajos chant. Beauty is before me. Beauty is behind me, above and below me. In beauty we make peace with the world, with ourselves, with each other. We walk out and find the beauty that surrounds us everywhere we look amid the star-made shadows of this and every shining night.

So be it.

MEDITATION
August 2011

In those early hours of morning mist
before the dull summer heat
burns through and lays us low
there is a fresh stillness to the world.
Bathed in condensation
the landscape draws a deep breath
as if waking to the new day,
and we, frowsy with sleep, rise to be with it.

Ancient rhythms around us resume
as we mull: what of this day?
One more day,
A gift we are powerless to measure
A compliment we are incapable of returning.
This day, this life.
As a chorus of bird song erupts,
we turn with new purpose to join it.

Beyond Tolerance
November 8, 2009

MEDITATION

By the ancient Persian poet Hafiz:

> Admit something:
> Everyone you see, you say to them, "Love me."
> Of course you do not do this out loud;
> Otherwise, someone would call the cops.
> Still though, think about this:
> This great pull in us to connect.
> Why not become the one
> Who lives with a full moon in each eye
> That is always saying,
> With that sweet moon language,
> What every other eye in this world
> Is dying to hear.

Adapted from *Man's Search for Meaning*, by Victor Frankl

In this passage Frankl describes an episode in his experience at a concentration camp during World War II:

We stumbled in the darkness, over big stones and through large puddles, along the one road leading from the camp. The accompanying guards kept shouting at us and driving us with the butts of their rifles.... Hardly a word was spoken; the icy wind did not encourage talk. Hiding his mouth behind his upturned collar, the man next to me whispered suddenly: "If our wives could see us now! I hope they are better off in their camps and don't know what is happening to us."

That brought thoughts of my own wife to mind. And as we stumbled on for miles ... nothing was said, but we both knew: each of us was thinking of his wife. Occasionally I looked at the sky, where the stars were fading and the pink light of the morning was beginning to spread behind a dark bank of clouds. But my mind clung to my wife's image, imagining it with an uncanny acuteness....

A thought transfixed me: for the first time in my life I saw the truth as it is set to song by so many poets, proclaimed as the final wisdom by so many thinkers. The truth—that love is the ultimate and the highest goal to which we can aspire. Then I grasped the meaning of the greatest secret that human poetry and human thought and belief have to impact: Our salvation is through love and in love. I understood how someone who has nothing left in this world may know bliss, be it only for a brief moment, in the contemplation of his beloved....

In front of me a man stumbled and those following him fell on top of him. The guard rushed over and used his whip on them all.... My mind still clung to the image of my wife. A thought crossed my mind: I didn't even know if she were still alive. I knew only one thing: Love goes very far beyond the physical person of the beloved. It finds its deepest meaning in one's spiritual being, one's inner self.

I did not know whether my wife was alive.... There was no need for me to know. Nothing could touch the strength of my love, my thoughts, and the image of my beloved.

SERMON

The moment comes late in the penultimate book of the Harry Potter series: headmaster Albus Dumbledor is explaining to a teen-aged Harry how it is that repeatedly he has managed to escape the murderous intentions of the villainous wizard Lord Voldemort. Though Voldemort has made a disciplined study of the most frightening dark arts of magic, Dumbledor says, there is one power that he overlooked that Harry possesses in surprising abundance: the ability to love. And in the final book the reader sees how the many ways that love has entwined these two opponents ultimately saves Harry from Voldemort's direct attack and results in the master wizard's demise.

Part of the genius of J.K. Rowling's immensely popular series is how she weaves through her elaborate story the threads of so many religious traditions, not to mention folk tales and fairy stories.

And so it is no surprise that her tale should identify love as the most powerful magic of all. For this, too, emerges from the vast storehouse of human wondering and imagining about the source of meaning in our brief spans, whether it be the Christian story of Jesus's love, the Muslim teaching of Allah's merciful care, the Buddhist bodhisattva's discipline of compassion, and so on.

How, then, am I to explain the cringe I often observe among Unitarian Universalists when the talk turns to the role of love in our religious life? I remember a couple years ago when I did a sermon series on our Unitarian Universalist principles. I observed that the Commission on Appraisal, an association-wide elected body, was studying the principles with an eye to possibly changing them, and I invited you to offer suggestions as to what you might add, remove, or change. Several of you responded.

Our member Mary Alm wrote that one word that she felt was conspicuously missing from our principles was "love." "How incomprehensible is it that we do not mention love anywhere?" she asked. "What the world needs now, not just for some but for everyone, what there's just too little of.... Love's gotta be a touchstone."

That line received a few knowing chuckles, and I agreed with her, suggesting how it might be added. I think Mary's observation, and, frankly, my own impetus in support, played a role in ensuring that the word "love" made an appearance in the mission statement that the Board of Trustees crafted last year with your help and approved at our annual meeting. By virtue, I suppose, of the natural rhythm of the sentence, "love" ended up as the last word of our mission statement. "We nurture individual search for meaning as we work in community for freedom, justice and love." As such, it assumes an anchor position, grounding our understanding of ourselves and our work as a congregation.

And yet, I know that for some of you this is treacherous ground. Words matter, and especially when it comes to religion they come freighted with all sorts of ancillary meanings. If we say that we as a congregation work in community for love, what does that mean? What else are we saying? After all, we gather in this place with no common frame of reference theologically.

Do we have anything like a common understanding of this love we say we are working for?

These are great questions that I hope we will find occasion to engage in many different settings. Today I'd like to offer some of my own reflections on what we might mean and why I believe we have placed "love" exactly where it belongs.

Let me begin with some thoughts about why the word "love" might push some of our buttons. We come to this church from many different places, some of us from church communities where "love" had a specific theological context.

They were communities of smiles and hugs and lots of talk about love. And yet, Sunday mornings featured sermons centered on a narrow understanding of that love and a narrow path to it. Questioning that understanding and that path put one outside of the love proclaimed in that community. And so, people left, carrying with them, often, the wounds of breaches with family or friends and no little amount of suspicion when the talk in church comes around to love.

Coming to this place, looking for a new start, they are wary of squishy words like "love" that can be twisted and turned against them. Better to shape our religious understanding with words that have sharp edges and clear boundaries. Steer clear of the touchy-feely stuff. I remember that a member of a congregation I used to attend would upbraid me when I took a turn in the pulpit as a lay person and would use the word "love" in my sermon. She said she didn't think that "love" was the right word to use in that context. A better word, she said, was "respect."

I understand the source of this woman's concern. Across the ages churches have been guilty of using the language of emotion to manipulate people: riling them up with doom and gloom, or lots of happy talk. This concerned the founders of the Unitarian movement in Boston during the 18th century, who saw the revival preachers of the Great Awakening peddling "emotional exuberance" but little in the way of religion that would be a source of hope in people's lives.

William Ellery Channing led the way, arguing for the central role of reason in religion, and that commitment has remained at our core ever since. And yet, Channing also argued that the point of religion was not so much to accumulate knowledge as to develop character. By character he understood living an ethical life but also devoting oneself to the larger good. And one developed character, he believed, by developing habits of heart and mind that put oneself in the disposition to act rightly.

There are without doubt many qualities that contribute to right living in a spiritually centered way, but with all due respect to my friend back in Milwaukee I believe that love is not only central, but foundational to them all.

Love, it seems to me, lies at the core of our identity, that spark within that makes us who we are. It is what drives the best that is in us, that connects us to one another and fuels our compassion. It propels not only where we put our hearts, but our intellectual curiosity and thirst for justice as well. When we talk about what we love, we talk about what connects us most deeply to who we know ourselves to be, to an essential truth within us. But it is in community, in the interaction of person with person, that love becomes an active force in our lives, one that grows in strength the more it is employed.

I have always felt that our Unitarian Universalist first principle is in essence the principle of love. In affirming each other's inherent worth and dignity we learn to appreciate each other and others in the wider world: having open eyes not only for each other's beauty and gifts but also our weakness, flaws and fears, and finding cause, not for judgment, but for compassion. We see between and among us a kinship. I not only accept you, I see in you something precious. Even when we err, we carry the seeds of forgiveness and renewal in that deep understanding.

If Hafiz is right, that we go about the world saying, "Love me," with our eyes, I believe it is this kind of love that we seek. Not romantic love, but a quality of regard from another that is beyond tolerance: a matter not of simply putting up with each other, but of recognizing that in how we touch each other's lives we are irrevocably involved in each other. That great pull to connect works on us, draws us in. And part of our work as a community is to follow it, to broaden and deepen it.

But it's also true that love puts us at risk. Each time we open our hearts we make ourselves vulnerable. It brings to mind words from a poem I received recently from a couple at whose wedding I officiated: falling in love as being like owning a dog.

> Love wakes you up all hours of the night with its needs. When it's cold outside it lies between you and breathes and makes funny noises.
>
> Is love good all the time? No! No! Love can be bad. Bad, love, bad! Very bad love.
>
> Love makes messes. Loves leaves you little surprises here and there and needs lots of cleaning up after. Sometimes you want to roll up a piece of newspaper and swat love on the nose, not so much to cause pain, just to let love know: Don't you ever do that again!
>
> Sometimes love just wants to go for a nice long walk because love loves exercise. It runs you around the block and leaves you panting. It pulls you in several directions at once, or winds around and around you until you're all wound up and can't move.

> But love makes you meet people wherever you go.
> People who have nothing in common but love stop
> and talk on the street. Throw things away and love
> will bring them back, again and again and again.
>
> But most of all, love needs love, lots of it. And in
> return, love loves you and never stops.

I want to suggest that this metaphor, amusing as it is for what it says about what goes on in relationships, informs our discussion as well. When we live so as to choose love as a first principle, we abandon the fiction that we are free-floating atoms, depending on no one and determining our own destiny. Instead, we understand that our destiny, our very being is intimately interlinked with all that is. We are drawn into the world's messes and tragedies, but also thrilled by its victories and awakenings.

It can feel overwhelming, leading us to wonder how much our hearts can possibly hold. And that is why we must learn, as every great prophet has taught, that love is a practice, a discipline. We must learn to hold both pain and joy, but not let either overwhelm us. We must take the time to get to know ourselves and learn to be present to others in ways that deepen our understanding and appreciation. We remember, after all, that the heart is a muscle and so is strengthened through exercise.

Love looks soft but is remarkably resilient, and in the end is source of the deepest peace. When I am confused, angry, possessive, afraid, if I have the presence of mind to take a breath and reflect on what love teaches me, I can regroup and find a way forward in peace. The bullies of the world consider love a push-over. The treacherous seek to use it to manipulate others. Tyrants see it as a sign of weakness. Not one of them understands.

Victor Frankl's awakening came amid the most horrid and degrading circumstances, slogging through icy mud, chained in a line of prisoners at a Nazi work camp. And still, bringing his wife's face to mind, he was able to tap into that source within him that gave purpose to his days. It was in love and through love that he was raised above the numbness that the camp's conditions had drilled into him. He found again the possibility of meaning in the world, and it saved him.

Now I have to add that this moment of awakening is not a place where one lives for long. We need to be careful of how and to whom we give love. We need to learn how to be with people of all kinds, how to engage difference and still find compassion. There is tough work to do and many years before it is completed. There are difficult circumstances to endure and little choice but to gut through them. We need to learn more, ask incisive questions, organize, and stay centered.

But we do this all from a grounding of deep appreciation and broad fellowship: in short, love. For us fragile, fallible folks, learning all that love has to teach is an unending task. We get fearful, frumpy and frustrated. We get self-righteous and insecure. We go trotting up dead ends and trip over foolish assumptions. We stumble, lose heart. We fall ill, we die.

And yet, in the days we are given, the time devoted to love and that which feeds love fulfills us as nothing else can. And in the hand that is held out in compassion, in fellowship, in love lies the hope for us all. The ancient Hebrew writers had the right idea: when it comes to making meaning in our lives, love is as strong as death.

And so I think we did the right thing in giving love an honored place in the statement that declares what we stand for and what guides our work here. We seek to provide a crucible, safe space where we might nurture each other in the journey of making meaning in our lives, confident that that work will embolden us to act in such a way that will advance freedom—freedom from oppression, from hatred, from fear—as well as justice that will achieve the reconciliation of all peoples, and love, sweet love: the glowing coal that longs for connection, what the world needs now, the spirit of life that sings in our hearts, that deepest, holiest force that joins us all.

May we have the courage and the strength to be guided by love, in love, through love in the days that we have, in this community that we make, in this blessed and beautiful world in which we live.

Meditation
November 2012

O, good heart, won't you take a moment and settle down?
Busy mind, busy life, settle down.
There, there, just sit, sit.
In this moment, as good as any,
let me be present to this space,
not awaiting, not hoping, not longing,
just welcoming, accepting.

Let me savor the sweet gift of being,
Scentless, tasteless, soundless, textureless,
And yet so full.
This snatch of eternity I inhabit,
Immense and intimate,
In the company of these companions,
Multitudes in each of them.
In this place, let my rising gratitude lie before me
As we enter the silence together.

WHAT WOULD THEODORE PARKER DO?
November 4, 2007

It is always a little perilous to reach back in history for exemplars of the religious life. The tendency is so strong to exaggerate for effect, to buff the profile and file off the rough edges so that the image we get is a bit superhuman, larger than life. I've found this to be true in our tradition with such figures as William Ellery Channing and Ralph Waldo Emerson on our Unitarian side, or John Murray and Hosea Ballou on the Universalist.

In this pantheon of our past, though, there is one figure who I find is consistently underrated, whose story often appears as little more than a footnote in quick summaries of our movement, and that's the Unitarian Theodore Parker. And yet, in his time—the 1840s and '50s—Parker was one of the most influential preachers in the city of Boston, regularly drawing Sunday audiences of 2,500 people—nearly 2% of all non-Catholics in Boston—and often many more.

Even more important is what he was famous for. At a time

when Americans were just beginning to waken to the emerging social ills of their growing nation, from lack of education to poverty and ill health, and most prominently the stain of human slavery, among American clergy Theodore Parker was arguably the most fearless, most tireless, most determined prophet of reform.

I have chosen Parker as my focus today as I continue my series this year intended to answer the questions arising from our strategic planning process: who are we, and who do we want to be? To remind you, I have already offered two propositions to answer those questions: We gather as a community to learn how to live what love teaches, and we invite and make room for the experience of wonder and the holy. Today I want to add to that list by suggesting that we regard ethical living and service to justice as religion's truest witness.

It is not all that we are about. Spiritual exploration and the search for truth and meaning require a good deal of inner work as well as time to engage each other and the world apart from the breaking issues of the day. But we do not fully inhabit our faith until we live it, until it guides how we interact with others and society at large, until it helps open our eyes to a larger view of the world and the duty we owe to each other, in fact to all humankind, and to the earth.

Parker was born on a ramshackle farm in Lexington, Massachusetts, the eleventh and last child of parents in their late forties. Though poor, the family boasted the pedigree of Theodore's grandfather, Captain John Parker, who, at the Battle of Lexington, famously told the colonists he commanded as the British regulars approached, "Don't fire unless fired upon. But if they mean to have war, let it begin here."

Parker enjoyed growing up on the farm, and all his life acquaintances would remark on his large farmer's hands. But his remarkable intelligence clearly set him apart for other work. He had a nearly photographic memory, a seemingly limitless appetite for reading—as a minister he compiled the most extensive private library in Boston—and eventually learned about a dozen languages.

Family connections found him a place at Harvard. He prospered there, but he had to follow a slower pace than most for lack of money, teaching in private schools between his classes. The ministry appealed to him at an early age. His mother was devout and influenced him strongly.

He told the story of being a boy and coming upon a turtle in the middle of the road. His first impulse was to grab a large stick and smash it. As he raised the stick, Parker said, he heard a voice inside telling him it was wrong, and he put down the stick. He recounted the incident to his mother, who told him that what he heard was the voice of God within him, and that throughout his life he would be on the right path if he followed that voice.

Parker's first settlement at a Unitarian church in West Roxbury came at a time when the Transcendentalist movement was first emerging, and he was intrigued by it. From his earliest days he had believed, as the Transcendentalists suggested, that religion "is deeply laid in nature and in the human heart." He came to meet and admire Emerson, attended meetings of the Transcendentalist Club, wrote for the group's magazine, *The Dial*, and was in the audience when Emerson gave his Divinity School Address at Harvard.

Parker, too, became drawn into the hubbub that followed, particularly around whether the Bible and its testimony of Jesus's miracles was essential to religious faith. For Parker, Transcendentalism affirmed that religion amounts not to a unique, divine revelation that we receive from the beyond, but to the process of awakening to essential truths that live within each of us.

Though an admirer and able scholar of the Bible, Parker felt that it had no unique authority. What it teaches, he said, "we could find out all by ourselves at some period of our lives." Its chief lesson, he felt, was what he called the essential nobility of human nature and our duty to one other. And yet, in his own day he saw little evidence that religion was at work on that task.

Christianity, he said, "nods over her Bible, and sleeps in her pew of a Sunday, while she makes slaves and keeps them, and strives to render the rich richer and the poor poorer all the week."

Parker's sermons took on an increasingly strident reformist tone, as he denounced the exploitation of labor, lack of education, and prisons that, he said, make more criminals than they mend. Parker was not alone among clergy in despairing of evil ways, but he was careful where he placed the blame. The injustices of society, he felt, were due far more to the selfishness of the strong than the failings of the weak. Human greatness was to be measured not by the fame or wealth one had accumulated, but by the service one had given to the world.

Ultimately, though, it wasn't a social reformist talk but an ordination sermon that raised Parker's profile and made him a figure of controversy for the rest of his life. The topic he chose for himself in the sermon was "The Transient and the Permanent in Christianity." Parker's candidate for the "permanent" was Jesus's teachings, words so compelling, he said, that they sewed themselves into the hearts of his followers, who created what he called a religion of "pure morality" that has endured ever since.

The transient, he suggested, was everything else: the clergy, the creeds, the cathedrals, even the Bible, with its many contradictions, and the person of Jesus himself. For it was the truth of Jesus's teachings, not any personal authority of his, that gave them their power. So, he said, "If it could be proved … that the gospels were a sheer fabrication, that Jesus never lived, still Christianity would stand firm."

It was, to say the least, an unorthodox point of view and quickly got him in trouble. Orthodox ministers hooted that Parker finally proved what infidels Unitarians were, and Unitarian clergy, in turn, shrunk from the criticism. Most stopped associating with Parker at all, and some even tried unsuccessfully to force him out of the ministers association.

As hurt as Parker was by this treatment, he didn't back down. And while the clergy were scandalized, the notoriety brought increasing numbers of visitors to Parker's church. In time Parker's friends began organizing for him to speak at a venue in Boston. They rented a theater, the Melodeon, and after about a year of Parker splitting his time between West Roxbury and the Melodeon, he resigned his pastorate to become minister of the newly formed 28th Congregational Society.

It was an unusual congregation, made up largely of middle-class Bostonians, evenly divided among men and women and, virtually unheard of at the time, racially integrated. The new location gave Parker more visibility, and Sunday attendance rose; eventually they had to move to an ever larger location: the Boston Music Hall.

Parker's hour-long sermons were earnest and artful, often packed with information—statistics on Boston's population and commerce—urging sympathy for the downtrodden and action by the privileged. But on no subject was his preaching more powerful than slavery. He came fairly late to the issue: it wasn't until the mid 1840s that he joined the abolitionists, but quickly he rose to become one of their most powerful voices.

Against those who insisted slavery was a Southern

problem, Parker argued that it was sustained by laws and commerce originating in the North. "Southern slavery," he said, "is an institution which is in earnest. Northern freedom is an institution which is not in earnest." His sermons and speeches emphasized that this "new crime against humanity" was corrupting the nation. Parker helped organize Vigilance Committees to protect fugitive slaves and even harbored them in his home, once marrying a couple before they fled for England.

Parker was clear on what he saw as the role of religion. Preaching on the occasion of his own installation at the Melodeon, he said that while the church exists to cultivate the heart, mind, and conscience, it should also "be the means of reforming the world." Churches, he said, may preach good will, "but every almshouse ... shows that the churches have not done their duty.... Every jail is a monument ... that we are still heathens ... and the gallows ... the embodiment of death, a sign of our infamy."

"It seems to me," he said, "that any church ... which aspires to be a true church must set itself about this business.... The church that is to lead this century will not be a church on all fours; mewling and whining, its face turned down, its eyes turned back. It must be full of the brave spirit of the day" demanding "as never before freedom for itself, usefulness in its institutions; truth in its teachings, and beauty in its deeds."

One hundred and sixty years later it's not a bad goal for any church, and one that this church can claim some pride in working toward. This morning you heard testimony to how some of our members are reaching out to men in the Buncombe County Jail. Just last night the latest edition of our electronic Social Justice newsletter, *The Flame*, from our member Cathy Agrella, appeared in my e-mail inbox, detailing some of the amazing work we are doing now and opportunities for involvement in the future. Among other things I learned that we led the pack, raising more money than any other group, in this year's Crop Walk. Choose your passion: environmental awareness, peace studies, anti-racist work, equal rights, economic justice, and so much more. There's a place for you.

Of course, social justice is just a part of what we're here for. We gather in worship each Sunday, and in classes, committees, choirs, covenant groups, and social gatherings. On our own, we study or meditate, practice yoga or tai chi. We sit with each other in sorrow, in crisis, or in need. There are many dimensions to the religious life, to the life lived with intention, integrity and love. One of them is how we answer the question, what will I do to live what I believe, or borrowing Albert Schweitzer's words, "How can I make my life my argument?"

There is no prescription to follow, no assigned path. We are each guided by our own gifts and our own predilections and circumstances to live as our values teach us to be of use, to find work, as Marge Piercy put it, that is real. In all that we do we can have no assurances that our best efforts will not be frustrated, disregarded or misunderstood. We can only know that we are acting out of our best selves, following what our hearts and minds tell us, that small voice, whatever its source.

We do, however, have the resource of community, a community committed to the inherent worth and dignity of all, to justice, equity and compassion. And joined as a community our strength is magnified.

There is no telling where the work that we begin will end. Theodore Parker had no way of knowing that his words in an antislavery speech describing democracy as "a government of all the people, by all the people, for all the people" would be immortalized two years after his death in Abraham Lincoln's

Gettysburg Address. Or that another of his images—that the arc of justice is long but it bends toward justice—would be adopted a century later by a 20th-century prophet, the Rev. Martin Luther King Jr.

Obscure as Parker is to most people today, his ideas and images still resonate. Only last January the commentator Bill Moyers cited Parker as "the Hound of Freedom who helped to change America through the power of the word." It is a power we each possess, in differing measure, to be sure, but true all the same. Our power is our voice, our capacity for action. Our religious heritage calls us to use them. For in using them, in living our truth, we draw closer to that center of integrity which gives our lives meaning.

We may follow different paths, find different stars to guide us on our way. But as we struggle for what it means to live an ethical life and to serve justice I want to suggest after this introduction today that we could all do a lot worse than asking ourselves the question, "What would Theodore Parker do?"

Meditation
March 2011

I woke today to torrents of rain,
battering the roof and windows,
pulse after pulse washing over us
as wind rattled the frames.
How thin are the shelters
we construct for ourselves!
No matter how stylish, how sturdy,
there is not one that some storm
could not reduce to sticks.
And so with our lives.
Brick by brick, we build our edifices
shaped by time, circumstance, luck,
each far more precarious than we guess.
And so, when storms come,
we weather them as best we can,
hoping they will just glow over,
or maybe pull off a shingle or two,
but knowing it could be much worse.
May this community be a shelter
against the battering of tempest,
and may our promises intertwine,
weaving strength into purpose and hope into our lives.

Minister's Musings
October 2007

It was a misty afternoon—not quite fall, though it felt like it—when I carried the bowl filled with water from our Water Ceremony down to the Memorial Garden. A pan was heating to a boil on the stove in our kitchen with water I had taken from the bowl and will use for child dedications in the year ahead. As I walked into the Memorial Garden I stopped before the brass plaques on our wall and silently read the names of church members whose ashes have been buried in our garden. Then I slowly poured the water that we had gathered over the area where the ashes of those dear folks are buried, saying simply, "We remember you."

I reflected as I walked back inside on how we as Unitarian Universalists struggle with ritual. Many of us came from religious traditions with rituals that felt to us like empty gestures or meaningless incantations. Historically our tradition has been wary of ritual as a way believers can be manipulated and oppressed. And yet we also are drawn to the power of words or gestures that connect us to what matters: people we love, ideals we hold dear, or a way of touching what our principles call "that transcending mystery and wonder, affirmed in all cultures, which moves us to a renewal of the spirit and openness to the forces that create and uphold life."

On that day I felt drawn to make a brief ritual of returning water to the earth in that special place. It reminded me of other rituals in our church life, such as lighting the chalice to begin each Sunday service and joining hands to sing our closing song to end it. We have discovered, I think, that it is possible to craft rituals that have integrity, that ground us in this world and connect us, one with the other, in the spirit of hope and love.

PART II

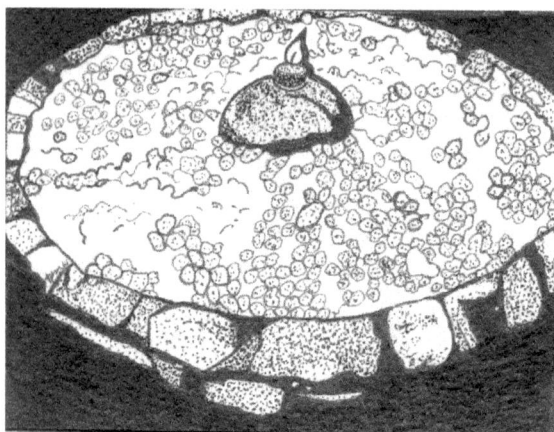

Boundless Love
September 30, 2012

Imagine sandy soil underfoot, the cries of gulls in the air. It is a Sunday morning, and a small crowd has gathered before a rough-hewn meeting house for the first worship service ever held there, even though the house itself has been standing some ten years. The speaker, a visitor, is invited to enter. His topic this morning: uncover the light.

Such was the scene 242 years ago today at a homestead along the New Jersey shore where one of the foundational stories of American Universalism unfolded. The speaker was John Murray, a one-time British preacher who had traveled to the New World to make a new start after worlds of heartbreak and disappointment back home.

His host was Thomas Potter, a farmer and a bit of a searcher and mystic. In recent years, he had become enamored with new ideas he'd been hearing about how all people might ultimately find salvation. He had been inviting visiting ministers to his house to talk about this, but his wife, Mary, had tired of these sessions. So he built this meeting house with the intention of hosting someone who could preach the gospel of universal salvation.

Murray had, in fact, aligned himself with an emergent Universalist movement in Britain, but left it after losing his fortune to debt and his wife and only child to illness. He only happened to meet Potter because his ship was grounded on a sand bar and he had led a party ashore to get provisions.

Potter, though, was certain that this meeting was no happenstance and implored Murray to preach in his meeting house. Murray insisted that he was done with preaching and just wanted to get on his way as soon as the wind changed. Potter persevered: "The wind will never change, sir, until you have delivered to us, in that meeting house, a message from God."

Murray finally agreed that if the wind did not change by Sunday he would speak. It didn't; Murray did, and he went on to become one of the leaders of what was to be the Universalist church. I expect that many of you have heard this story. It is a standard part of introductory classes in our churches.

And why wouldn't it be? It's irresistible: not only the serendipitous meeting of Murray and Potter, but the fact that the ship Murray sailed on was the *Hand in Hand* and Potter's property was on Good Luck Point.

In fact, it's so compelling a story that it's easy to exaggerate its larger importance for us. Historians of our movement remind us that Murray was not the first Universalist to come to America, nor was his message unique. A French Universalist, George De Benneville, preceded him by at least three decades, and at about the same time a wave of German Baptists called "Dunkers," who emphasized atonement for all, had settled around Philadelphia. These were likely some of the people who influenced Potter.

Murray went on to help found the first Universalist church in America in Gloucester, Massachusetts. And at around the same time, independent of him, a Universalist movement was emerging in the hill country of southern New Hampshire where some of the most important leaders of the church were developing.

And from there it spread with early settlers into the west and the south in the form of unlettered preachers who took to the road with nothing but a Bible in their saddlebags. Universalists emerged in North Carolina in the 1820s and here in the western mountains by the 1850s. This Saturday I will join members of our congregation on a visit to Inman Chapel, out in Haywood County at the foot of Cold Mountain, a remnant of those early Universalists.

I say all this not to diminish Murray's importance but to make a larger point. What we call Universalism was not the invention of one person. It has popped up in many places across the ages, often among people who had no particular religious training other than their own reading and faith. Early in the Christian church it was condemned as a heresy—confused thinking of the uninitiated—but across history it continued to emerge, a tough weed that church fathers never seemed quite able to pull. And beyond Christianity it has emerged as what you might call a "universalizing" approach to religious faith in other traditions as well.

I think there's a reason for that, for it seems to me that this "universalizing" tendency is really an innate human response to that depth dimension in all of us.

Much criticism of religion tends to focus on the divisiveness that often attends religious life, the formation of mutually exclusive sects and all the ways that religious bodies divide humankind into sheep and goats. This, too, I must say, I believe also to be an unfortunate tendency within us, a clannishness that pits peoples against one another.

But there is another way, a way that may yet save us, a way woven into our natures and ingrained in this tradition and others that affirms the human tendency to see an essential commonality in our fellows amid our diversity. It is a way that makes room for many strains of thought and belief while affirming a common bond among us. It paints faith not as a narrow path with dangers we must fight at every hand but more like a river that draws us to the sea.

A poem by the Universalist Edwin Markham tells it best:

He drew a circle that shut me out –
heretic, rebel, a thing to flout.
But love and I had the wit to win:
We drew a circle and took him in.

"Love and I had the wit to win." So, what is this love?

Let's turn for a minute to Hosea Ballou, whom you heard quoted earlier. As important as Murray may have been as a founder, Ballou qualifies as one of Universalism's most important thinkers and theologians. And that's curious given that Ballou was almost entirely self-taught. But it was in the major work of his life, called *A Treatise on Atonement*, that he laid the groundwork for how American Universalism would develop.

What made Universalism controversial in its early years was its insistence, against Calvinist claims that perdition awaited all but the elect, that, to the contrary, there is no hell and all people would be saved at death. There was some disagreement among Universalists about whether you might need to spend some time in purgatory to work off your sins. But in the end, they insisted, no sin was so terrible as to merit eternal damnation and eventually all would end up in heaven.

This was by far the minority position among clergy and church-goers. Most, including some Unitarians, felt that evil-doing in life sent you to the fiery place at death, and without that threat hanging over people's heads, they didn't believe you could expect them to do the right thing.

Early Universalists, like Murray, insisted that Jesus's death on the cross assured that all believers would be spared. But Ballou rejected the notion that Jesus's death was a sacrifice that freed all from sin. A loving God, he said, doesn't require the sacrifice of Jesus or anyone. That's not how God works. There is no need for hell after our deaths, he said: we create enough hell for ourselves by our own folly, hubris, and error in life.

God, he said, only calls us to love, to love all things, to give ourselves to love: a love that we don't have to seek out or search for, a love that is available to us here, now. You get a flavor for his cadences in the reading. "There is nothing in heaven above, nor in the earth beneath, that can do away with sin"—with all the ills and evils of the world—"but love."

And then here he turns to the evocative language of the Song of Solomon: "We have reason to be eternally thankful," he says, "that love is stronger than death, that many waters cannot quench it, nor the floods drown it; that it hath power to remove the moral maladies of humankind." Not to say that this is an easy task. "O lover, thou great physician of souls," he writes, "what work hast thou undertaken."

In Ballou and many of the early Universalists we can see that universalizing tendency at work. As I said, many of these Universalist enthusiasts lacked much in the way of formal education, a fact as much as anything that kept early Unitarians in their high pulpits from making common cause with them, to the detriment of the Unitarians.

Their preaching was often rough-hewn, but it needed to be, given the audiences they were speaking to—often a few families gathered in the living room of a farm house—and their competition—often fire-breathing evangelists. Their sermons were tightly argued, hewing closely to the Bible, but also full of fervor for this expansive vision of the divine, a vision that, while centered in one context, opens the door to a wider one.

One thing that intrigues me in this passage from Ballou's *Treatise* is how he begins moving beyond the conventional language of personified deity. Pronouns fall away, and with the poetic language of that sacred song he seeks to evoke a broader image: love itself as a force in the world.

I spoke earlier about the depth dimension of our experience. It's a place where we as Unitarian Universalists often struggle, where we've found that words can fail us or trip us up. And so we turn to the experience itself—however we frame this, what is happening in me in my life as I live it? What do I observe in my life that is true?

The poet May Sarton wrote about how it feels when that the breakthrough, the epiphany that gives us that answer happens. "Now I become myself," she wrote. "It's taken time, many years and places. I have been dissolved and shaken, worn other people's faces." Now, she says, "to stand still, to be here, feel my own weight and density! All fuses now, falls into place from wish to action, word to silence, my work, my love, my time, my face."

Most of us can name such experiences, when the world suddenly came together, where we knew wordlessly who we were, where we fit, what we are called to. For me, the clearest example of this came with the birth of my children. Their appearances immediately created a tug on my life. However I may have been drifting, I was righted and a connection was created. I have not always been as responsive or responsible as a parent as I wish I had, but when I have given myself to the love they kindle in me, I am not only fed deeply, but their presence in my life has changed me, opened me, made me better. I have not done anything heroic to make this happen other than simply align myself with the power and beauty inherent in this connection.

I look at it as one of those moments when love became active in my life, when it grabbed me and pulled me forward. And, just as May Sarton described it, all fused in my life, fell into place "from wish to action, word to silence, my work, my love, my time, my face." I can't say I've always lived in that state, but I've experienced it and I aspire to it. I'll bet you've experienced it too, whether or not you've had children or anything like it.

There is a force that moves us, within us, that can rouse us from stupor, from selfishness, from fear. Sarton describes it as "one intense gesture of growing, like a plant." It is a universalizing force that is blind to difference and that helps us see to the heart, to the human, to our inherent wholeness.

Seeking a name, let us call it love: not soft, simpering love, but love such as Mary Oliver imagines it, like a black bear rising from sleep, headed down the mountain, flicking the gravel with black fists, its tongue like a red fire, touching the grass, the cold water, sharpening its claws against the silence of the trees. A force of nature, of perfect love, breathing and tasting as it rumbles down the mountain

I think it's true that, as the poet suggests, whatever else the details of our lives may be—in her case, her poems and glass cities—there is also inside us this powerful truth, this dazzling wonder, our capacity for transformative love that expresses the best that we are. It is what gives us the courage to widen the circle when our fears counsel us to keep it closed. It is a mysterious current whose origins elude us, yet that tugs us relentlessly toward wholeness and hope.

It may be that in the end John Murray deserves the credit he has received. After all that had happened to him, it took great courage to mount the pulpit once again before those strangers in that meeting house on the Jersey shore. With breakers crashing in the distance, it seems that he must have felt his own scarred heart opening once again. And it's likely that he was preaching to himself as much as to the congregation when he advised them to put aside their worries and fears, open themselves to boundless love, and uncover the light within.

Meditation
September 2010

Why does it have to be so hard sometimes
this being in relationship, being in community?
Why do we sometimes so willingly
injure each other's tender hearts?
The cutting comment, the thoughtless gesture,
the angry word, the dismissive remark.
These, and worse, pepper our days
More often than we'd like to think.
Out of the moment, away from the interaction
we affirm to ourselves, and with sorrow,
this is not who we are.
If only.
If only we could fix it, so it never happened.
If only we could erase it and start over.
But wounds to the heart don't magically vanish,
though they can be healed.
And it is us, the injurers, who carry the balm.
The ointment of apology goes far.
The oil of compassion soothes wounded flesh,
The elixir of humility wakens a dulled spirit.
May we all learn to be such physicians to each other.

STANDING UP FOR EQUAL RITES

March 19, 2006

I had a light-bulb moment the other day as I was mulling over this issue of marriage equality. I thought about the awkwardly phrased ad in the *Asheville Citizen-Times* a little over a week ago from a cluster of Baptist churches, full of vague code words and tortuous readings of the Bible that condemned homosexuality. And then I thought about the faces of people gathered in this sanctuary in opposition to that ad the following Saturday, gay and straight, young and old, speaking from their hearts about people they loved, some of them angry, some of them fearful, some of them sad, but every one of them determined. And then it dawned on me: we're going to win this. I can't say how soon, but there is now no doubt in my mind. The campaign for marriage equality not only should, but will, prevail.

Now, before you conclude that I'm really losing it, let me share with you the direction of my thinking. Some of you may be familiar with the book, *Tipping Point*, by Malcolm Gladwell. Gladwell describes the fascinating way that social change sometimes can happen surprisingly quickly. The metaphor he uses is an epidemic. Like a virus, an idea can insinuate itself in a population and quickly gain a following. Whether it actually catches on, Gladwell says, depends on a couple of key principles.

One of those is what he calls the "stickiness factor." That is, there's something compelling about this idea, something that draws people to it, that works on them over time. Another is what he calls "The Law of the Few." This is to say, it is not necessary to convince a majority of people to accomplish social change. Only a small number of people are needed, but they must be people in different niches and subcultures who work their social connections, who gather and distribute information, who touch the chords of sympathy in others, and, most important, who believe that change is possible.

What occurred to me suddenly is that we are nearing the tipping point on this country on marriage equality. Yes, the forces lined up against it are formidable. Yes, we may lose battles in the short run. Still, I believe—not merely hope—but firmly believe that we are nearing the time when all loving couples, irrespective of sexual orientation, will have their unions recognized as having equal status under the law.

Notice, though, that I said "nearing." Hard fights and disappointments lie ahead, and dedicated work will be needed by those of good will who hold to the worth and dignity of every person to make it happen. But every sign I see says the change is coming, and not because we wish it so but because it simply is inevitable. Those Baptist preachers with their scare words are fighting a losing battle, beating the drums of fear in the face of an epidemic that is spreading rapidly from heart to heart.

Perhaps part of the reason I am making my point in this dramatic way is that I myself have experienced a clear shift in my thinking recently, my own tipping point, which I will tell you more about later. For now, let me say that for some time, while I supported equal rights to marriage, I tended to temporize:

Yes, of course, it's the right thing, but, gosh, the Christian right is so powerful, there's no way it will change, and, gee, maybe we could work out some limited compromise like civil unions and maybe some day, long come the millennium, we can see if there might be support for marriage.

Nope. No more. I have come to realize that while I have been temporizing, a sea change has been under way. After generations of being cast as pariahs, gays and lesbians are joining the mainstream in this country. Yes, archaic rules still govern some institutions like the military and a few churches, but in neighborhoods, workplaces and at family dining tables, gays and lesbians are finding a level of acceptance greater than at any time in history, and winning allies in places where it never before would have seemed possible.

I understand that many people still need to be careful. We know the story locally of Laurel Scherer, who lost her job as a photographer at Wolf Laurel ski resort when her employers learned that she and her partner, Virginia, had married. My brother Terry, who sang here at church last fall, is open to family and friends about being gay. But when he went out to interview for administrative positions at several private schools, he made sure to skirt the fact that he shares the apartment he gives as his address with his partner, Gary.

The "stickiness," to use Gladwell's term, of same-sex marriage begins with the day-to-day experience that heterosexuals have with gay or lesbian family members, friends, bosses, or neighbors. The fear of difference dissolves as we get to know and care for each other. And as gays and lesbians come to feel braver about introducing their partners to heterosexual friends or co-workers, those friends and co-workers learn to experience them as a couple with many of the same struggles and stresses, joys and epiphanies that they have.

We are all still negotiating this, some with more success than others, but it is a rare heterosexual these days who will claim not to know a homosexual, and that alone goes far to defeat many of the fearful objections to same-sex marriage. Nothing defeats the impulse to demonize so well as the face of a family member or friend.

What has happened is that the terms of the debate have changed. We are not talking about "special rights" for some distant class of unknown folks. We are talking about people we know and the people they love. We are, to use the phrase of Bill Sinkford, president of the Unitarian Universalist Association, standing on the side of love, and there is no downside to that.

Still, it is true that we are left with some huge hurdles to achieving equal marriage rights, and two of the biggest come in the form of the church and the state. We saw in the *Citizen-Times* ad how homophobia has been enshrined in some religious traditions. Some churches remain a powerful voice opposing equal marriage rights, but others are a growing force for change.

Shortly after arriving here in 2004 I discovered the North Carolina Religious Coalition for Marriage Equality, which is organized locally as a group calling itself People of Faith for Just Relationships. It is clergy and lay people from at least half a dozen denominations who recognize the injustice of laws that prevent same-sex couples from marrying. They are acting not only as advocates but as a healing presence in this community, helping their own parishioners and others of good will understand that the true call of faith is toward reconciliation, not the division of humankind.

I am proud to join with them, recognizing as well that our Unitarian Universalist Association has been a leader in working for the civil rights for gays, lesbians, bisexual, and transgender people. Our clergy have been performing wedding ceremonies for same-sex couples for decades, and in our congregations we have been engaged in serious work to recognize and unlearn homophobia. This church, too, has done that, and more than ten years ago voted to become a Welcoming Congregation.

I am proud of the work that we and other progressive churches have done on this issue, and the role that all of us are taking to shift the religious dialogue so that churches open their arms to and bless the commitments of gay and lesbian couples. But I am also aware that the center of this debate belongs outside of the sanctuary. It is important to remember, after all, that the rights that concern same-sex couples are those conferred not by the church, but by the state.

Part of what may cause confusion on this point is the curious role that ministers, like me, play in this process. I wonder if you know that last year when you ordained me in this church you formally made me an agent of the state. It's true. Simply by virtue of being ordained by a recognized church I am entitled to sign, and therefore legalize, marriage licenses. At the end of the wedding ceremony, after vows have been said and Lohengrin has been played, the marriage is not legal until that moment in a back room of the church when I affix my name to the couple's license.

It is, when you think about it, an odd state of affairs in an otherwise secular nation that clergy—unelected, unappointed by any governmental body or official—are given such a right. And yet here we are. Perhaps it's little wonder, then, that clergy, accustomed to pronouncing couples husband and wife, feel they can pronounce to the state who should and should not receive a civil marriage license. In fact, it is none of their business. I almost wish it were, for then I could sign licenses for same-sex couples irrespective of what state law says. But no.

Churches may set whatever rules they wish for what couples they will marry, but they have no say-so over who may receive a civil license. What we are dealing with here is a civil right, a fundamental right to equal treatment. And so, we must deal with the state.

It is here where advocates of same-sex marriage get especially gloomy. Across the country, legislatures controlled by religious conservatives have made constitutional amendments limiting marriage to a man and a woman a high priority, and so far are having a distressing number of successes.

It troubles me, but still I can't help but believe the right's urgency on this issue is driven by its own perception of the approaching epidemic I cited earlier. They see a narrow window while they are in power when they hope to lock in regressive restrictions before the tide turns against them. I suppose I can't blame them for trying. I would were I in their position. But in the end, it won't matter.

Why do I say that? Well, once you get past the right's homophobia, the reasons they cite for opposing same-sex marriage are surprisingly flimsy. We are told, for example, that same-sex marriage will somehow "diminish" the institution of marriage, or that it doesn't serve the purpose of procreation.

The Rev. Fred Small commented recently about efforts to "defend marriage." "I have to tell you," he said, "as a minister, I counsel a lot of married couples who are struggling. They're struggling with money, parenting, communication, sex—but no one has ever come to me and said, 'My marriage is in trouble because of the homosexual agenda.' Defending marriage is about putting more faith, hope and love into our marriages, not about excluding people from its legal protections."

The fact of the matter is that our society is well served whenever two people of whatever sexual orientation join in a committed relationship. It gives stability to their lives, and to all who depend on them. It gives them a stake in a civil society working toward the good of all.

And as for procreation, if that were a requirement for marriage, it would prevent many heterosexual unions as well. For those same-sex couples who do want children, the same options are available to them as to heterosexual couples.

Now, let's turn to what same-sex couples lose under the status quo, or even so-called "civil union" legislation. Why marriage, after all? What's the big deal? The benefits of marriage are something that heterosexuals like me take for granted, yet they are woven throughout our lives.

They range from special tax treatment to Social Security, Medicare, and Medicaid protections. Someone added it up and discovered 1,138 ways in which federal law favors marriage. And that's just federal law. We haven't delved into protections in state law or private protections in areas like insurance. This is the practical reason why civil unions could never be a substitute for same-sex marriages. Marriage is too interwoven into our laws, our culture. Civil union would always be a second-class designation. But there's more.

If I were rushed to the emergency room, no one would question the right of my wife, Debbie, to be there. A same-sex couple has no such assurance, and indeed gays and lesbians have died alone, with their partners parked in waiting rooms, because no one would recognize their right to be present with their loved one.

You see what I mean by an epidemic of the heart? Under no circumstances can that be a just thing. It doesn't matter what Bible verses you read, or whether you are uncomfortable with the notion of two people of the same gender in bed together. It is simply wrong. It tears at you. It sticks to you.

You don't have to listen to much of this before you before an agent of Malcolm Gladwell's "Law of the Few," before you are ready to work your social connections, to learn and get yourself savvy on this subject, before you learn to touch the chords of sympathy in others, and, most important, before you, too, believe that change really is possible.

I told you earlier of the tipping point I had experienced personally on this subject. It's hard to describe exactly how this came about, but the best parallel I can give you comes from a dissenting opinion in a U.S. Supreme Court case on capital punishment that I heard about twelve years ago.

In the decision, Justice Harry Blackmun, long a supporter of the death penalty, announced that he had changed his mind and would oppose it. He detailed all the ways that the state tries to assure that those charged with capital crimes are treated fairly but concluded that despite all of them, in his words, "the death penalty remains fraught with arbitrariness, discrimination and mistake."

And so, he concluded, "from this day forward, I no longer shall tinker with the machinery of death.... Rather than continue to coddle the court's delusion that the desired level of fairness [in how the death penalty is applied] has been achieved, I feel obligated to simply concede that the death penalty experiment has failed."

My own experience is on a par with Blackmun's. I have decided that I will no longer to tinker with the tortured logic of injustice. I will not coddle the illusion that we can support and honor same-sex commitments short of marriage. Justice and the source of our own personal integrity demand equal recognition. And for support of this, I turn to my own theological center, my recognition that we are fundamentally relational beings, that it is in relationship that the person we were meant to be is realized, that whatever the holy is, it is embodied in how we live the truth of our deepest love.

So, yes, count me among Gladwell's "few" on this issue, ready to lend my hand to spread this epidemic, may it be virulent.

As one contribution I can make to the cause, I have decided to join the Rev. Joe Hoffman, pastor of First Congregational United Church of Christ in Asheville, and cease acting as the agent of an unjust state. From now on, until our laws are changed to guarantee equal rights to all, I will no longer sign the licenses of couples I marry. The sole exception will be a few couples whose weddings I have already agreed to officiate.

I have also been authorized by my colleague, and our member, the Rev. Pete Tolleson, to tell you that he, too, will no longer sign marriage licenses.

I won't speak for Pete, but in my case this does not mean that I will no longer conduct weddings. As I told you last year, I consider the decision of two people to commit themselves to an enduring relationship of love and trust an event to be celebrated, supported and blessed. I happily accept my role and responsibility to assist members of this church and others—gay or straight—to create and carry out such ceremonies. But I will not act as the state's agent to legalize those unions that the state approves. I will, however, inform those who are lucky enough to be able to have their marriages legalized how to exercise that option. The process, I can assure you, is not onerous.

I must tell you that one of the influences that led me to this was our daughter Anna. Anna is a member of Arlington Street Church in Boston, one of the leading Unitarian Universalist Churches in the fight for marriage equality. In 2004, when the Massachusetts Supreme Court legalized same-sex marriage, Arlington Street hosted some of the first same-sex weddings, and Anna, a member of the choir, got to ring the church's bells for some of them.

Last fall, when Anna and her boyfriend, Langdon, decided to get married they were conflicted on where to hold the ceremony. They had always thought about getting married in the chapel at Kalamazoo College, where they had met and both attended. But having watched and cheered the gains of same-sex couples in Massachusetts they didn't want to apply for a license in a state where gays and lesbians are refused that privilege. So, they decided to compromise: late this summer will obtain their license in Massachusetts, and then gather with their respective families and friends for the wedding in Michigan.

I don't mean to be casual in tossing off the difficulties surrounding the needed change on this issue. The fears and prejudices that inform those in opposition are deep-seated and strong. There will be times when confrontation will be needed to achieve progress; but there will also be times when compassion is the key. We are not talking about just winning a political battle here. We are talking about opening people's hearts. And it is my heart that tells me we will win.

It is my heart that sees past the circumstances of people's lives, past all the differences you can enumerate, and sees in each person something sacred and great. It is there I locate my hope, knowing all the ways we disappoint each other, the cruelty of which we are capable, and all the same insisting that the heart's call will emerge, will carry enough of us who are brave enough to follow it to widened sympathy.

I invite you to bring your heart and join us. If you are female and I am male, it will not matter. If you are gay and I am straight, it will not matter.

What matters, in Marjorie Bowens-Wheatley's words from our affirmation, is that we join as brothers and sisters, that the pain of our aloneness be lessened and we work to build a community that offers hope and restoration.

So be it.

PART III

DARWIN'S DOUBTS
February 5, 2006

The year is 1831 and the subject before us is a 22-year-old man: son of a doctor, seminary student of middling ability with a love for the out-of-doors and a passion for collecting creatures of all sorts. A kind but reserved fellow, he has just shipped out of Plymouth, England on Her Majesty's Ship *The Beagle* on a trip to survey the coast of South America. His shipmates are curious about him, most of them regarding him as a type they've seen before: one of those privileged young men setting off on adventure to "find themselves."

Connections through family and professors at Cambridge had gotten him an interview with the ship's captain, Robert Fitzroy, a man who himself is on the young side to command such a ship and sought a companion to keep him company. Though wary of the young man at their first meeting, Fitzroy later warmed to him and agreed to sign him on as naturalist on the voyage. Elated at the news, the young man, Charles Darwin, who had never been off the British Isles and rarely far from the copses of southern England where he trapped bugs of all kinds, had crowed, "Woe unto ye, beetles of South America." And so, now off he heads into the stormy, grey waters of the Atlantic.

One hundred and seventy-five years later, we look back

at this shy but persistent naturalist, trying to grasp what it was that prepared him for insights that would transform our understanding of ourselves, our world, of life itself.

It may seem odd, in light of how the world works today, and ironic, given the religious controversy that surrounds Darwin's work, that the *Beagle's* captain would have engaged a student in ministry as his ship's naturalist. In the 19th century, though, much of the grunt work of science—collecting, cataloguing, and so on—was done by amateurs, and many of those amateurs were clergy.

The life of many a country parson at the time was not especially demanding and, whatever was going on in the parish, there was usually time during the week for other pursuits. Many enjoyed bracing hikes in the countryside. This is, in fact, an important part of what made the ministry attractive to Darwin. Having flopped at medical school, he was resigned to becoming the dutiful preacher; to suffer through Sundays as long as he also had time to tramp the countryside and collect his beetles.

For most clergymen, though, it was more than the blithe air that they sought on their hikes: it was the opportunity to be amid what they took to be the wonder of God's creation. Everywhere they looked, from bluebirds to black bugs, they found beauty and intricacy that to them argued for the marvel of the creator's work. Darwin in his early days felt this way too. Remember that sciences we know today as biology, physics, or chemistry began as branches of theology.

An important text on this subject in Darwin's time was a book called *Natural Theology* by the Rev. William Paley. Paley famously argued that if you chanced upon a watch lying on the ground, you would come to the conclusion not just that someone owned the watch and had accidentally dropped it, but also that the watch surely had a maker. Even if you had never seen a watch before, the intricacies of its workmanship and construction would convince you that it must have been conceived and built an intelligent entity. Likewise, Paley wrote, when we examine nature, the vast and subtle complexities of design that we find carry us to the inescapable conclusion that only the infinite intelligence of the creator himself could fashion such things. (Have any of you heard an argument something like this recently?) What today we call science was, then, for many at the time merely another form of devotion.

One of the most amazing of these self-described acts of devotion was the work a century before Darwin of the Swedish botanist Karl von Linne, who wrote under the Latin name Carolus Linnaeus. In the hope of gaining a glimpse of the plan of the creator he sought to work out the relationship of all living things. He divided living things into kingdoms, then classes, orders, genera, and species, a system so beautiful that later it was adopted by all Western naturalists. (Other categories have been added in years since, but Linnaeus's system of classification is still used.)

Linnaeus felt that his system described the living world as God had created it. So, each classification all the way down to species was fixed firmly for eternity. In later years after studying the many variations that occur within species, Linnaeus began to wonder if there might be occasions when species could be altered. And in time various mavericks, including Darwin's own grandfather, Erasmus Darwin, argued that species could adapt over time. But the position of the orthodox remained fixed.

As the author Jonathan Weiner put it in his book *The Beak of the Finch*, each of Linnaeus's types was considered "a specimen of God's thought at the moment of Creation. Every detail of every beetle had a sacred message if we could learn to read it; even the lowliest worm had begun as a thought in the mind of God."

This was a perspective that Charles Darwin, despite his grandfather's opinion, largely embraced as he sailed from Britain for points south. His goal was not to challenge orthodoxy, but to gather as many different creatures, plants, fossils, and other unusual artifacts as he could.

Actually, there was one controversial theory that Darwin was toying with at the time. It was contained in Charles Lyell's book *Principles of Geology*, which he brought with him on the *Beagle*. Lyell argued that most geologic change took place, not in great catastrophic events like earthquakes and floods, but as the result of continuous processes within the Earth. Even more, he insisted that, contrary to most teaching at the time, the processes of nature had no connection with events in the Bible and had nothing to do with what theologians considered God's plan for perfecting the Earth.

Darwin found that his observations of landforms supported Lyell's approach. Even more, he discovered fossils of long-extinct lizards that raised for him what in his early writings he described as "the mystery of mysteries": why some species disappear and how new species emerge. To accommodate this, creationists at the time argued that the coming and going of species was God's work. He would decide when one species would wink out of existence and when it was time for a new one to appear, but Darwin wasn't convinced.

Of all the *Beagle's* ports of call, the one that both unsettled and intrigued him the most was the Galapagos Islands. He was taken aback by the extraordinary number of new species he found—plants, birds, tortoises, and more. Not only were they different from plants and animals on the mainland, but they varied from island to island: in some ways they were as close as cousins and in others quite separate. More and more, not only did he doubt that species were fixed, but he also began wondering what might be driving the changes. "One is astonished," he wrote later in his first book, *The Voyage of the Beagle*, "at the amount of creative force, if such an expression may be used, displayed on these small, barren, and rocky islands."

Upon returning to Britain and showing his collection to experts, he found his doubts only more deeply confirmed. In several cases, plants or animals he thought at first might just be variations of one another were in fact separate species and seemed certain to be linked by common ancestors. Within a year or so he was planning in his notebooks a work on what he called "the transmutation of species."

Darwin was willing to entertain the idea of evolution. What he lacked was a theory to describe how life evolved. Two sources gave him the grounding he needed. The first was Thomas Malthus, who had pointed to how in nature plants and animals produce more offspring than can survive and warned of poverty and famine unless human populations were controlled. Darwin realized that if there were more offspring than an area could support, the ones who survived would be those best suited to the environment.

He also found inspiration in agricultural breeding. Just as pigeon breeders select those individuals with attributes they want to preserve for future breeding, so in nature individuals with qualities best suited to the environment where they lived would be selected by surviving and passing their winning attributes to their progeny. That was the heart of the mechanism Darwin discovered to explain how life on Earth evolves.

Almost 150 years later, the details of evolution are still debated. How exactly do new species emerge? Is evolutionary progress slow and steady, or does it proceed in fits and starts?

And there is much more besides. Darwin himself was well aware of the furor his work would evoke. Describing his conclusion that species change over time in a letter to a friend, he confided, "is like confessing a murder." And in a sense it was.

Darwin's work argued against the cozy vision of a world conceived, created, and watched over by a loving, infinitely wise God, and seemed to substitute for it a chaotic image of self-seeking creatures, ourselves included, who had to scrape and contrive for every advantage. It opened a vast rift between science and religion, consigning the Book of Genesis to myth and poetry, and while it didn't necessarily unseat God as a force in nature, it certainly made him more of a bit player in the affairs of the world. At the same time, though, it also opened an exciting new possibility: that life on Earth is more than clever machinery guided by a master hand, but something with agency of its own.

Darwin ventured that the "creative force" that he found at work in the Galapagos archipelago was not imposed from without but arose from within. He didn't know how—it has taken the discovery of DNA and the genetic revolution now before us to begin unraveling that puzzle—but he showed us where to look: not afar but in the very stuff we are made of.

Darwin's work was greeted with howls of outrage, even despair, by those who saw in it a grim portrait of the world, one seemingly devoid of purpose and meaning, where self-seeking and cut-throat opportunism were rewarded and tender concern was trampled underfoot. I am drawn, though, to Darwin's own words in his masterwork, *On the Origin of Species*. Far from being a negative force, he says, "natural selection can act only through and for the good of each being." Remember in our reading from that book earlier, he spoke of natural selection as a kind of force that is "daily and hourly scrutinizing throughout the world ... rejecting that which is bad, preserving and adding up that which is good."

We have to be careful, of course, of how we understand that "good." It is not a purposeful good, such as the unfolding of a divine plan that Charles Lyell's contemporaries envisioned. It is, in essence, the most basic good: endurance, survival, continuing on. And, contrary to the image of evolution, we have learned that endurance often requires not so much self-concern as cooperation and collaboration among species.

What we know about life is that it is, above all else, tenacious. It works its way in wherever it can and employs whatever strategies it can to survive. Those strategies may benefit or inconvenience other living things—we humans, for example, rejoice in strawberries but curse kudzu—but strategies will endure as long as they benefit the thing itself. And there is another curious thing about the good promoted by the process of evolution. In the long run, it has come to serve not only individual species but all living things. Millennia of evolution have resulted in a spectrum of life on Earth of extraordinary diversity woven into a vast web of interlocking relationships.

So intimate are these connections that some have suggested we might even consider the Earth itself, or at least its sheath of life, a self-existing body. If so, this raises the question of what role we as human beings might play in that body. Do we represent a growing intelligence and empathy that will bring about a new flowering, or an infection that an immune response of fever and attack will seek to eliminate?

It is possible, of course, to carry this metaphor too far. As much as we have learned about how life works, there is so much more that remains a mystery to us. What we do know is that the conceit of our predecessors who regarded humans as specially entitled to dominion over the earth was mistaken. Our own survival depends on our better understanding our relatedness with and obligations to other life. What gives us exalted status, if we can be said to have any, is our ability to select for, to choose those behaviors, those strategies that will serve the essential good of all life: endurance, continuation, survival.

"I call to heaven and earth to record this day against you," said Moses in his final sermon to the nation of Israel as he looked across the Jordan River to the promised land that awaited them. "I have set before you life and death, blessing and curse; therefore choose life that you and your relations shall live."

The choice for us is much the same, though the relations we have to account for form a far wider web than the one that Moses imagined. Will we choose life and bless the Earth, or follow ways that only serve to diminish it and, in time, life itself?

Darwin returned from his five-year trip on the *Beagle* keenly aware that a quiet life of parish ministry would not suit him. Not only was he swept up by all that he learned into the newly emerging world of professional science, but he was troubled by new doubts about many of the church's teachings that before he left had seemed so clear.

In time Darwin lost much of his early religious faith, but that was the result not so much of his thoughts on evolution as the death of his ten-year-old daughter Annie in 1851, eight years before *On the Origin of Species* was even published. He could find little comfort in a God who could permit such a thing. After that, he never again concerned himself in any significant way with religion.

Darwin was happy, though, to let this new work, following the thread of life's emerging, consume the rest of his days. There was enough there to fuel his awe, his admiration, his hopes. And that is certainly true of science today.

The controversy drummed up by modern-day creationists

and William Paley's intellectual inheritors, the proponents of "intelligent design," spills a good deal of ink and generates political heat, but it is irrelevant to the work of science. Evolution as conceived by Darwin and worked out by generations of biologists is not just a theory; it is an established fact, proven over and over again.

It has given us a tool for understanding our origins and how all living things are related. It has also helped us appreciate how as inheritors of billions of years of flourishing diversity, a capstone species in terms of our intelligence and complexity, it is incumbent on us to be stewards of the living Earth.

As Darwin himself reminded us in the final paragraph of *On the Origin of Species*: "There is grandeur in this view of life ... that whilst this planet has gone cycling on according to the law of gravity, from so simple a beginning endless forms most beautiful and most wonderful have been, and are being, evolved."

So be it.

Meditation
December 2012

Dawn comes slowly when the light is less,
and with the cold, sleeping world
I am reluctant to waken.
Like chilled honey on a spoon
tipped over a restorative cup of tea
my slow thoughts adhere and protest
before slipping into a waiting world.
How good to have the warmth of community
awaiting me at this fallow time.
How good at this waking
to leave the shadows of sleep
and find blooming before me
the brightness of day,
the wonder of beauty,
the gift of love in my life.

THE WAY WITH NO GOD: ATHEISM AS A RELIGIOUS PATH

November 6, 2005

READINGS

From *In the Beauty of the Lilies*, by John Updike

The Reverend Clarence Arthur Wilmot felt the last particles of faith leave him. The sensation was distinct—a visceral surrender, a set of dark sparkling bubbles escaping upward.... He was standing, at the moment of the ruinous pang, on the first floor of the rectory of the Fourth Presbyterian Church, wondering if in view of the heat he might remove his black serge jacket, since no visitor was scheduled to call until dinnertime, when the Church Building Requirements Committee would arrive to torment him with its ambitions. The image of the chair's broad assertive face ... slipped in Clarence's mind to the similarly pugnacious and bald-crowned visage of Robert Ingersoll, the famous atheist whose *Some*

Mistakes of Moses the minister had been reading in order to refute it for a perturbed parishioner; from this perceived similarity his thoughts had slipped with quicksilver momentum into the recognition, which he had long withstood, that Ingersoll was quite right: the God of the Pentateuch was an absurd bully, barbarically thundering through a cosmos entirely misconceived. There is no such God, nor should there be.

From a sermon, "If Not God, What?" by the Rev. Kendyl Gibbons

What we are hungry for is not God. "God" is only a name we give to one way of trying to describe the experience that comes when we are someone, simply, mysteriously filled; when we get past our distractions and illusions and pride, to the reality upon which existence itself is founded. Something about that reality is a needless, gracious gift; the eternal surprise that there is anything instead of nothing, and that the anything includes us and our awareness.

Something about it makes us understand that we are painfully finite; that our time is limited, our individual abilities and understandings are limited, that we are parts and participants in a project that endures beyond us and is greater than ourselves. And something about that reality calls us, allures us, demands of us that we grow into all the wisdom and justice and love of which we are capable, because that is the fulfillment of the deepest reality of what we are.

SERMON

In his novel *In the Beauty of the Lilies* John Updike depicts the Reverend Wilmot's loss of faith as a kind of hollowing out of his life. As the promise of God the creator ebbs away, so does much of his joy. As the theological puzzles, the habitual mental contortions that occupied so much of his working life evaporate like so much morning mist, Wilmot feels an immense strain lifted. And yet, Updike writes, "the depths of vacancy revealed were appalling.... There is no God. With a wink of thought, the universe had been bathed in the pitch-smooth black of utter hopelessness."

To many a believer, such is the fate that awaits anyone who would deny God's existence: a dull, empty, disenchanted life, devoid of meaning or hope, a pointless plodding toward nothing greater than personal extinction, or worse, a fiery fate for eternity. It is a grim picture that has been elaborated on time and again from many a pulpit, to the point that many who identify themselves as atheists often find themselves pitied, shunned, or distrusted.

Indeed, for many the very title of this service is nonsensical. For most believers—and I'll wager many atheists as well—to speak of atheism as a religious path is a contradiction in terms.

Like John Updike's Rev. Wilmot, most of those who abandon or steer clear of a belief in God, abandon or steer clear of religion entirely. And that's fine. My point today is not to say that atheism necessarily is a religious path, but that it can be: that one can develop a path of meaning within community that is satisfying, provides a grounding for ethical action, and satisfies the human need for depth and connection without reference to God or any supernatural being.

In our lives, each of us develops a religious perspective that arises out of our upbringing and our responses to the world. Over time that perspective shifts and grows as we grow, sometimes deepening, sometimes undergoing a dramatic change. It is a tenet of our tradition that none of these perspectives offers a final answer, none embodies absolute truth. Each is a partial answer to the quandaries that we confront in our lives, to our need for hope and meaning.

We also believe that each of us benefits from open dialogue, from challenging each other and being challenged in a spirit of love. And so, throughout this series, let me invite you to leave yourselves open to being stretched, to listen with sympathy and respect, so that we might deepen our understanding of each other and also model the kind of wider acceptance and interchange so needed in our fractured world.

Rev. Wilmot notwithstanding, the experience of most atheists is not one of despair. Instead, for most the notion of God is just not part of the equation in how they organize their world.

Constructed as it is, the word "atheist" suggests an opposition to the belief in God. Strictly speaking, it means the denial of the existence of God. And, certainly there are angry atheists who see it as their purpose to refute or belittle the concept of God, but for most this active opposition is not part of their belief system. They are simply satisfied to accept the world of their experience—the birds, the bees, the oceans, the stars—as all there is. Supernatural beings or forces are not something they experience, and they don't play into it.

The Rev. Khoren Arisian, long-time minister of the First Unitarian Church of Minneapolis, tells of experiencing a hurricane when he was a boy. His mother, he said, was awestruck by what she saw as the fury of the Lord and sought to protect him, but Arisian said it never occurred to him to be afraid. He was fascinated and excited by all the chaos of which Nature was capable, and he traced his own naturalistic worldview to that experience.

Throughout his youth, he said, God was a concept that he never found of much use. In later years as he himself was drawn to the study of religion, Arisian said he came to the conclusion that the image related in the Bible's Book of Genesis had the order reversed. It was not so much that humans were made in the image of God, but that we had envisioned a God in the image of humans. He saw God as a concept constructed to serve humans' needs and offer them a favored place in the universe.

Then, as he continued his religious studies, he learned that for many that quaint, homespun image of the deity had faded in favor of an image of God as immanent in the world, a creative process or unknowable ground of creation. This was a very different concept. Indeed, he noted, in advocating such a view, the 20th-century theologian Paul Tillich had dismissed all conventional concepts of God as idolatrous: false images that detract from God's true nature. Yet, such a move, Arisian said, raises questions about what in the end we understand God to be, and certainly what role he may have in people's everyday lives.

In the end, Arisian said, he decided that "for me the continuous use of that word (God) to represent humanity's vast and varied spiritual questing is, though understandable, nonetheless confusing and gratuitous. Nothing is gained, and I believe much is lost, by the emotional insistence that God and religious be coterminous. The word becomes simply more misleading as history goes on."

Many atheists hold a similar perspective: for them, the concept of God doesn't add anything. It merely confuses the picture. Unlike Rev. Wilmot, they do not view the world as empty or devoid of meaning because there is no God in it. The world as it is, is enough. All the meaning there is, as well as beauty and wonder, can be found there.

That's all well and good, the theist responds, but what guides you to act ethically, and how do you deal with death? That first question was once put to a friend of mine this way: If you don't believe in God, why are you good?

The premise behind that question is that without a rule-maker dictating what is right and wrong, or the threat of cosmic punishment, we have no reason to act ethically. Indeed, in the mind of many a believer, atheism is the first step on a road to a libertine lifestyle. And yet, if history is evidence of anything, it is that a belief in God is no sure ticket to ethical behavior. The litany of horrors perpetrated in the name of faith ought to be enough to give pause to anyone insisting on such a thing. As the Rev. Donald Jacobsen once wrote, "There is a belief in God that says that we should beat our swords into plowshares, and a belief in God that says we should praise the Lord and pass the ammunition. There is a belief in God that commands us to love justice and mercy, and there is a belief in God which sanctifies almost every injustice and oppression."

My experience is that a more reliable indication of moral behavior than an avowed theological belief is one's ability, as evidenced in one's actions, to see beyond the end of one's nose, the recognition that each of us owes a duty to others.

Last year our members Clark and Anna Olsen gave me a lovely calligraphy that you will find hanging in my study that illustrates the fundamental precept underlying ethical action that reaches across all cultures. In the West we know it as the Golden Rule, but you will find similar language in the teachings of Hinduism, Buddhism, Confucianism and more: treat others as you would be treated.

We sometimes understand this as a principle of reciprocity: be nice to me and I'll be nice to you. But it also suggests something more. Implied in the Golden Rule is the understanding that each of us has value: not because of who we are, or what we do. Our value is inherent, not contingent. We are not required to justify our existence. The fact of our humanity is claim enough for a duty owed to us by other humans.

Now, why should this be? The theist points to the belief that we are all God's children. God chose to create each of us, to give us life. Who are we to argue whether we have value? God has already decided that question. The atheist, though, has no independent authority to point to, no source that somehow confers value, and is left, instead, with the simple fact of existence itself. I cannot know why or how I came to be. I am here. That is enough.

I have a place in the vast, interwoven web of existence, and that is a source of value in and of itself. The same may be said of my fellows and the many beings with whom we share this time on Earth. Down to the chemistry of our DNA we share a heritage and a destiny. We are bound up with one another, and that association, that embrace of mortality, gives us all a natural affinity, and that affinity, whether we call it divine or arising from our own evolved natures, it is root of all ethical action. We may give it many names, but in the end all names are reduced to one: love. Love is not just passion; it is the source of hope, of courage. It is that which gives life meaning and purpose.

We don't always look at things that way. We take things for granted, sometimes mistake ourselves as having greater importance than others, or consider that our needs should trump theirs. This is a mistake that theists, atheists, and any other stripe of believer make. The corrective, however we frame it, is to bring us back to that first principle: the recognition that the interests of others bear on us; we have a duty larger than just to ourselves.

Okay, the theist says, now tell me about death. If there is no God to receive you in loving arms, what happens? In the 1960s, the folk singer Pete Seeger complained that he was often asked to sing at funerals but always was dissatisfied at not being able to find exactly the right song to express what he called "the situation," his estimation of what we're talking about when we talk about death. And so he wrote his own, a funeral song he titled "To My Old Brown Earth," and these are the words:

> To my old brown earth and to my old blue sky, I'll now give these last few molecules of I. And you who sing and you who stand nearby, I do charge you not to cry. Guard well our human chain. Watch well you keep it strong as long as sun will shine. And this our home keep pure and sweet and green, for now I'm yours and you are also mine.

I've thought a lot about the nonbeliever's reply to death in recent weeks as we have experienced the death of my father, Jack, and of Debbie's mother, Elizabeth. Both would qualify as some stripe of nonbeliever. My father's views, which he mostly kept to himself, were a kind of religious naturalism. In his eulogy of my father yesterday in Florida, his best friend described my father's beliefs with words of Albert Einstein to the effect that the world as it is holds wonder enough for us all. Over the years, Jack would listen to the theological debates of the ministers in his family, but it was not where his true interest lay. For that you would have to join him in the garden.

Debbie's mother was always clear about her beliefs. Though raised Roman Catholic, she was from early adulthood an adamant atheist, with no use for God and no use for religion. She was aware of how involved Debbie and I were in Unitarian Universalist churches, and while she was tolerant of what we told her, they certainly held no interest for her. You can imagine, though, that when I left journalism, a field she admired, for seminary, Elizabeth was thunderstruck. What on earth had come over me? We had some good discussions in the ensuing years, and I think reached something of an understanding. Next week I will be honored to officiate at her memorial service in Princeton, New Jersey.

Elizabeth and Jack both came to the ends of their lives bravely, concerned less about what would follow than that they end their lives in the company of those who cared for them. And it was that which those of us who attended them paid heed to.

I thought Debbie captured the spirit of those times best with a prayer that she said came to her mind as she was out walking one day in Princeton while hospice volunteers were seeing to her mother. She was trying to think of how she could best be of help in her mother's last days. The words that came to her, which she agreed to let me share with you, were these: May love guide my hands; may love guide my words; may love guide my actions.

And so it did. Love guided us and our families throughout those difficult days, despite our mourning and grief, and guides us still. And whether it was of God or a deep source of caring within each of us, it was enough; whether it led them to their ends, to the fires and ashes of their last molecules that soon will join the good brown earth or passage to something else, it was enough.

The end, after all, awaits us all, and whatever our faith, uncertainty must surround that moment. Atheist or theist or however we frame the state of things, we rue the day. But to meet that moment held in some way in the embrace of love offers comfort one can be sure of.

I reflect on the words we heard earlier of Kendyl Gibbons,

who succeeded Khoren Arisian at the Minneapolis church, about that hunger we all experience, that existential yearning for meaning, for belonging in this all-too-brief flicker of life to which each of us is treated.

There are moments, she said, when each of us comes to feel "somehow, simply, mysteriously filled; when we get past our distractions and illusions and pride, to the reality upon which existence is founded." We use different words to speak of those moments, those blessed glimpses of clarity that, in Gibbons's words, "call us, allure us, demand of us that we grow into all the wisdom and justice and love of which we are capable."

God, mystery, the essence of our humanity: however we frame it, it is the assurance that finite as we are, we are also part of something great, that our existence is a precious gift: a gift that fills us and holds us and affirms us. And that's enough.

To Have and To Hold
May 29, 2005

A couple of months ago I arrived at church to find a message on my voice mail from our eldest daughter's boyfriend, Langdon, asking simply that I call him on his cell phone. Langdon hasn't made a habit of calling me—in fact this was the first message from him I had ever received—so I was curious what this might be about. When I reached him, he came to the point quickly: he wanted to know if he could have my permission to marry our daughter.

Langdon and Anna met at college, have known each other for about five years and have been dating for about four. Now living together in Boston, they are each two years into graduate study and building a committed life together. What is more, they have a wonderful emotional bond that is apparent to anyone who spends any time with them. If ever two people were suited for marriage, these two are. And so, when the time came, I didn't hesitate to give him my blessing. But his call also prompted me to reflect on this complex, sometimes baffling institution of marriage and what we make of it today.

We long ago passed the time when parental permission was

expected to precede what was once known at the plighting of troth. And yet, what touched me in Langdon's gesture was not only the respect that he extended to me, and Debbie as well, but also how it spoke to the seriousness with which he took this important step in his and our daughter's lives.

We are, I think, at a turning point in how we regard marriage in our society. Certainly, the debate over marriage has gained a prominence it hasn't had in years. And what's interesting is that on both ends of the spectrum, while the two sides differ radically in their opinions, there is consensus on one point: marriage is important. Where they are divided is on the question of why.

At one end are religious conservatives who have set their sights on marriage as the guarantor of human virtue. And, of course, we are not talking about just any marriage. They mean the wedding of a man and a woman for the purpose of raising a family, where the father works and heads the household and the mother stays home and raises the kids. This model is still widely promoted in our culture, even if it represents a small minority of the actual marriages in our country. Nonetheless, we are assured, it is "traditional," an arrangement ordained by nature. This is rhetoric we are familiar with, even if its logic is a bit strained. The arrangement I just described may be "traditional" in the memory of people now living, but in the course of human history it is, in fact, a fairly recent innovation, barely more than one hundred years old.

E.J. Graff, in her Beacon Press book, *What is Marriage For?*, points out that during most of Western history marriage was more a business transaction than anything else, a way to ensure an orderly transfer of property from one generation to the next or to ensure the presence of enough hands to get the work done.

Certainly there were tender feelings between husband and wife and parent and child, but it wasn't until the late 1800s that people came to regard affection between two people as the main reason for marrying and the nurturing and raising of children as its central task. And as for roles of the sexes, until the rise of the Industrial Revolution, husbands and wives were more often partners in labor: the woman handling the books, buying for the business, or selling merchandise while the man worked in the shop or the field.

The model of marriage that conservatives identify as traditional may be familiar and therefore comforting to some, but it is hardly ordained by nature. What is more it has also been an tool of oppression, of women forced into roles that never fit them, enduring abuse, domination and disrespect, of men numbed and hollowed out by societal demands and expectations. Behind the veneer of many seemingly "normal, traditional families" lies a good deal of grief, doubt, sadness and shame.

At the other end, the suggested solution to these ills has often been to either steer clear of marriage itself or negotiate a looser arrangement that avoids many of the entanglements of the traditional model. So, we had the "open marriages" of the '60s, where dalliances outside of the marriage bond were deemed okay.

A few years ago there was something called an "unmarriage" going around. As I saw it described, it was sort of like a marriage but without the legal formalities, intended for those who either couldn't get married, or had political reservations about marriage, or who weren't quite ready for that level of commitment. One "unmarried" couple in New York, a man and woman, reported even holding what they called "a commitzvah" where vows were exchanged and wine was shared. The man said that although it wasn't exactly what the families had hoped for, they were glad all the same. "My mother was very happy," he said. "She was like, 'I'll take whatever you're going to give me.'"

All this has changed in a dramatic way with the debate over the legalization of same-sex marriage. While on the one hand it has set the alarm bells ringing on the religious right, the self-appointed protectors of traditional marriage, it has forced those of us on the religious left to rethink our attitudes toward marriage and, in E.J. Graff's words, what marriage is for.

It has shifted the subject of the debate over marriage from social policy to civil rights. Over the centuries rights and privileges that grant social recognition and legal protection to marriage have accrued as a way of honoring the power and importance of those relationships both in our individual lives and in the fabric of society.

We are blessed to live in a time when the truth can finally be spoken that same-sex couples are equally deserving of that recognition. We are a ways from achieving that, it is true, but I take courage and comfort from the growing understanding that such recognition that such recognition is right, fitting and just.

The same-sex marriage debate has helped us see that marriage is neither the fulfillment of nature's plan nor some anachronistic holdover from an outworn paternalism. It is an ever-evolving expression of a fundamental human need, the need for relationship, and not just any relationship: relationship of depth, of trust, relationship that calls us to our best selves, that helps us live the love that is deepest in our hearts, relationship that fills and completes us. The covenant of marriage has its flaws, its peculiarities, but it is the best way we have today of proclaiming such a relationship and having it honored and respected.

In weddings where I officiate, I often make the point that

the vows that two people make to each other in marriage are unlike any other commitment they will make in their lives. The "troth" that they are "plighting" or pledging literally means not love or eternal devotion but good faith: promising to stick with another, to be true to them in all the ways that life finds them. That means not only sexual fidelity, but also honesty with each other about who they are and what matters to them. It means in a larger sense staying "engaged" in the relationship long after the wedding ceremony has passed.

The declarations of love, as heart-warming as they are to hear, in the end are not the real deal. How two people care for each other and how they express that will change. What marriage stands for is commitment, commitment not just to the promises articulated on the wedding day but to seeing the best in the other whenever possible, to respecting and nurturing the emotional bond between two people.

The word "troth," after all, has its origins in the Old English word for truth. More than anything else, marriage is about truth: the truth between two people, the mutual intent to be in relationship and to bring the best they are into that relationship, to have and to hold one another through whatever may come.

I have conducted nearly thirty weddings and unions so far in my ministry, and each has differed radically from the others. I began with a couple I had never met before: a special education teacher in her forties and a school principal. The teacher had figured she would never marry, but after helping the principal grieve the death of his wife, struck up a relationship that grew into love. We held the ceremony in her father's home overlooking the farm where she grew up in Eden, Wisconsin. (I've always liked that I conducted my first wedding in Eden.)

Then, not two months later came a pair of college sophomores who planned to marry in a hall overlooking Lake

Michigan in Milwaukee. One-time high-school sweethearts, they were so young it frightened me. They assured me, though, that marrying young was a pattern in their families, and it would work out. I hope that proved to be so.

There have been services before hundreds in churches and banquet halls, and informal ceremonies before a dozen or less gathered in a park gazebo or in someone's backyard. Young or old, gay or straight, they came with hopes and fears, and a light in their eyes when in sight of their beloved. Each of them has amazed me.

I'll be honest that sometimes I'm not sure as they stand there in their rented tux and corseted dress how many of the words that I and they are reciting they actually hear. And yet, there they are, their eyes glistening, their hands shaking. Something is happening here, and it is changing their lives.

And as formulaic as it sometimes is, I still find myself moved, wanting to celebrate: that two people came to a point in their lives where they took the brave risk to lead with their hearts, to let go for a minute of the "lonely me" and commit to a relationship as deep as the sea, rowing toward that long falls that Mary Oliver imagines plunging and steaming.

I recognize, of course, that making such a commitment offers no guarantee of its success. It can be hard to know when you need to stop rowing into a relationship and turn around and get out, when health, self-regard and compassion require that you leave. I expect there may be those of you here who are wondering in your own lives if it is time for a turn. It is some of the hardest work we ever do to struggle in those relationships to which we have given ourselves most deeply. It is out of respect and dedication that we invest ourselves in that struggle, hoping for a resolution, a meeting of minds and hearts. Sometimes it can be found, sometimes it cannot. In the end, we must choose that which will preserve our selves and our integrity. In the meantime, we seek out the solace to be found in the larger circles of caring in our lives.

And I need to acknowledge that not all of us end up meeting our needs for relationship in a long-term, committed partnership. Some never find that person; others lose that person and find they cannot be replaced. That doesn't lessen the fundamental need. It only means we need to find other ways to meet it, through friendships, associations: even here at church.

Our tradition, after all, puts relationship at its center. We welcome the experience, learning and understanding that each of us brings, but we make meaning in community. We become wiser, deeper, more compassionate the more we engage with others and share who we are and what is of worth to us.

Now, as for my daughter's wedding, she has already informed me that she will not prevail upon me to officiate, and I think it is a wise decision. It will be a day when I will need to be just dad, riding herd on my own surging emotions and everything else that such a day is sure to bring with it.

But I think if I had words to offer, they would be something along the lines of what Wendell Berry wrote in the reading we heard earlier: the giving of ourselves in marriage must be an unconditional giving, for in joining ourselves to another, we join ourselves to the unknown. Neither can know for certain what it will be or where it will go. It is going where the two of you—and also time and life and history—will take it. You do not know the road. You are committing yourself to a way.

A very Taoist thought, when you consider it. A relationship is not so much a thing as a way, a path of your own that you walk with purpose and with discipline. It is not the straight and narrow, drawn or dictated by others with their yellow lines and yield signs. It is the way of your heart, unfolding as it must, in partnership with another. Finding a rhythm, a pattern that works takes time, learning how to bend and grow, to recover from your missteps and then improvise some fancy footwork together.

Yes, marriage is important for loving souls, whatever their gender, because it is a way of representing, of giving voice to that greatest response of the human spirit, the reaching out to another in fullest relationship.

I found myself reflecting on this some weeks ago after getting home from a particularly trying wedding. It was one of those events where just about everything seemed to go wrong, but in the end the ceremony came together, and there was a sweet sincerity to it that buoyed me despite all the frustrations.

Reciting these events to Debbie, she stopped me at one point and said, "Dance with me." I found something slow, the first track of an Eva Cassidy CD. As we came together on the deck I closed my eyes. "Will you stay with me, will you be my love, among the fields of barley?" The music drifted on. Our steps slowed. We moved almost as one.

Ever renewing, ever renewed, we dance where our hearts take us, each coupling moving to a rhythm of its own, none of us, as Anne Morrow Lindbergh put it, loving the other in the same way always, and yet still on the path, still committed to the way.

Meditation
May 2007

Out of the mystery beyond knowing and into our lives our children are born, precious strangers with whom we share the most intimate ties.

It is our duty to welcome them, to guide them, to nurture them.

Even as we count every finger and toe, gaze into the wells of their eyes, and stroke their impossibly soft hair, we are daunted by the responsibility of their care.

And so, with love we bring them into our lives, our families, our communities, our world.

Life is busy, their needs are many, demands on us grow, and time is so short.

Here we gather for support and consolation, to complete the circle of care, to mentor, to teach, to laugh with, to cry with, to celebrate with courage and love.

And then the journey moves on. Our children leave our homes and make places in the world. The ties twist and stretch and yet endure.

Here we affirm the circle of love, where we each might care and be cared for, where we might stand with each other, living out of our best hopes and for our best selves.

Minister's Musings
May 2008

Driving up to Boston a couple of weeks ago to see our newly born granddaughter gave me a lot of time to reflect on the many transitions that life deals to us all. So much of what goes on in the early part of our lives is about individuation, about defining who we are and how we will engage the world. The visual image that comes to mind is a rising arc. If we are lucky, we find a place, a role that fits our gifts and who we are: the right occupation, the right kinds of relationships, and families, too, if we follow that path. It may take a while and there may be some hard bumps along the way, but we find an identity that satisfies us, or at least that we can make peace with.

Eventually, though, it seems to me that we come to a point where that rising arc turns and, again, if we are lucky, our lives come to define something like a circle; we find completeness in our days. Part of what happens when the arc turns is that our perspective shifts. What we do, what concerns us is less about us, about that identity we have spent so much energy defining. Instead, our perspective widens and we appreciate in many ways our wider connections. Many spiritual traditions speak of this transition, which they often associate with eldering. Eldering is not just the aging of the flesh; it is a recognition of the deepening of wisdom available to us all, letting go of what we have long taken to be individually ours and understanding ourselves more to be part of a communion of being. It is no longer achievement that drives us but completion and the possibility of giving some legacy to the future.

It is presumptuous, I know, for me to speak of such things, months away from just my 55th birthday. And yet our granddaughter's birth has given me some intimation of what that perspective might be. There is much more that I hope to contribute in my life, but as I held and rocked that tiny child I felt a tug that connected me in a way I never knew before to another rhythm, older and deeper than myself. I saw myself as a link in a chain extending farther than I can fathom into the future, and a chain not just of being but also of hope and love. May that be my legacy.

PART IV

FAITH IN A SEED
November 18, 2012

The winter of 1856 in New England was hard and long. From January through March in Concord, Massachusetts, the snow depth was never less than sixteen inches, even in the open, undrifted fields, and temperatures never rose above freezing. In the attic writing room in his family home, though, Henry David Thoreau recorded only delighted fascination with this midwinter chill. Watching the snowflakes, he wrote, "how full of creative genius is the air in which these are generated ... Nature is full of genius.... Nothing is cheap and course, neither dewdrops nor snowflakes."

This was about two years after Thoreau's book, *Walden*, was published and his own creative genius was turning to a new project. This time, instead of seeking to record of how to live deliberately on his own in a cabin in the woods, he would focus on cataloguing in as close detail as he could the natural world in the setting that surrounded him. He hoped that this project might help him root out the organizing principles that made the natural world not just a compendium of curious beings, but a community.

The Concord area had been lumbered over years before, and the forests were reestablishing themselves. On his walks, Thoreau's eye was drawn to the succession of trees that emerged, and he hoped, in his words, to "learn the language of these fields."

It's worth remembering that in the 1850s the way that biologists would have framed this "language of the fields" was closely tied to theology. The predominant view among scientists was that the species of all living things were fixed and unchanging, and that God brought them into being over time according to a specific plan of creation.

When species were discovered or emerged in unexpected places, they were viewed as an example of what was called "special creation," an act of God to unveil that species "spontaneously" in that place at that time. It was viewed as impossible—in fact it was an affront to God's plan—that species could be thought to have changed over time.

Thoreau was familiar with all this. He'd been admitted to scientific societies. He had even collected samples for prominent scientists and attended their meetings. But he was deeply skeptical of this line of thought. Years ahead of reading Darwin, Thoreau's own observations persuaded him that it was more likely that natural processes were guiding the changes he saw. But he needed data to tease this out.

Beginning in 1856 his journals began filling with the minutest details: observations on how trees succeeded one another in fields, how seeds of birches and pitch pines were scattered, and what animals were carrying them or burying them across the forests. He tore apart birds' nests and inventoried their contents; he dissected the droppings of crows.

His notes paint the picture of a man both intense and puckish who was absorbed in the world around him. In the passage you heard earlier he tells of mounting hilltops to tear off heads of thistle seed, rip them open, and toss the silky seeds into the wind, then standing, his vision fixed, as they floated like balloonists over the valley before him.

He describes collecting touch-me-not seed pods that, in his words, "go off like pistols on the slightest touch, so suddenly and energetically that they always startle you. They shoot their seed like shot. They even explode in my hat as I am bringing them home."

This attention to seeds was an interesting turn for Thoreau. In *Walden* he closed his first chapter, the one on "Economy," wherein he described his project to live alone in a cabin in the woods, with a parable of sorts. He told of a wise man who was asked once why, of all the celebrated trees in the flower garden of Sheik Sadi of Shiraz, none was called free, except for the cypress, which bore no fruit. The wise man replied that that was because the other trees were tied to the cycle of seasons. So, part of the year they were fresh and blooming, and part of the year they were dry and withered. The cypress, meanwhile, was free of this cycle and so was always flourishing. "Fix not thy heart in what is transitory," Thoreau writes. "Be a free man, like the cypress."

Yet, later in life when Thoreau began his draft for a work that he intended would sum up his observations on "The Dispersal of Seeds," a work he never finished, he quoted a different source. This time he cited the Roman orator Pliny, who said that trees that bore no seed were regarded as sinister or unhappy and were considered inauspicious.

That's quite a shift. In *Walden* the cycle of fruiting and withering served as a convenient metaphor for the quiet desperation of getting and spending, production and consumption that he felt governed the lives of his fellow town folk. The goal in his trip to the woods, he said, was "to live deliberately, to front only the essential facts of life." His aim was to live like the ever-flourishing cypress, free of the beholden entanglements of the world.

In his study of seeds, though, he had a different purpose and learned a different lesson. Seeds taught him that none lives alone and that purpose in life was to be found not so much in brave living as in generative living, in creative living. Success was to be found less in what one achieved in life than in what one passed along. And so, the tree that bore no seed, that had no gift to give to the future, was "unhappy."

A couple of years before his death at age 44, Thoreau did read Darwin's *On the Origin of Species*, and he was cheered to find many of his own leanings confirmed. In some of his last published writings he was one of the first Americans to applaud the evolutionary view of life.

Rather than being guided by some eternal plan, it was now plain, life on Earth was making it up as it went along, with creatures and plants of all sorts emerging and disappearing in the fullness of time. For Thoreau, it was an exciting vista that kept him fully occupied, even as illness took its toll. He had come to the conclusion, he wrote, that "the very earth itself is granary and seminary, so that to some minds its surface is regarded as the cuticle of one living creature."

It's an amazing image and one that resonates strongly with our own contemporary sensibilities. We hear it in Alison Hawthorne Deming's encounter with the insect collector. There, she and he conclude that, in her words, "it's wrong to think people are a thing apart from the whole, as it we'd sprung from an idea out in space, rather than emerging from the sequenced larval mess of creation."

It is something we don't particularly notice until our subjects—butterflies, skippers, mosquitoes and honeybees—are lined up in specimen boxes. Then suddenly we can see it—the way things adapt over time, guided by no particular hand but shaped in how they bump and jostle each other, in how the possibility that they carry emerges in the world. Each thing carrying within itself the ability in some way to shape the whole—a vast granary of life that gives rise to an unimaginable variety of beings.

But Thoreau goes further and calls the earth "seminary" as well—an instructor in the nature of the holy. The comment is surely in part a dig at the traditional instructors of religion whom Thoreau had little use for. But I think he had a serious intent in that comment as well.

The faith that a seed teaches is that the organizing principle in life is inherent to it, not imposed from without, and it is connected across generations and across the earth. Life supports, feeds on, and generates life.

Nature is full of genius, he wrote, a genius that is emergent and ever renewing as life itself evolves, one generation after another. It's a genius we honor this time of year with both the bounty at our table and the wonder with which we view the faces gathered there. We each take part with our place in the ever-renewing circles of relationship that join us across generations. Our tables become a place to appreciate both the marvel and the promise that we each bring and the links we offer to ongoing life.

The faith of a seed also teaches us, as Miguel de Unamuno urged, to shake off the sadness that sometimes arises from the circumstances of our lives, circumstances that can leave us feeling isolated or alone, aimless, purposeless. For, each of us bears a gift for the world, a germ of possibility, a way that we might be used to realize something great.

"To live is to work," the poet writes, "and the only thing which lasts is the work; start then, turn to the work." Like a seed we are realized, we are brought fully to life by how we grow.

"Throw yourself like seed," he writes—scatter great handfuls widely. Put what is living in you in the furrows as you go. Leave what is dead behind. Find a rhythm. Don't let the past weigh down your motion as you move up and down, back and forth across the fertile earth.

This was the image that Thoreau dwelled on in his final years, of the genius of nature scattering us and all beings widely that we might land in some fertile spot, put down roots, send up our tender leaves and in time bear the fruit that is ours to give.

And in the end as we watch it move like thistledown drifting in the breeze, who can say where we might deposit the precious freight of our living and loving at last?

Meditation
November 2007

As chill winds blast the last autumn leaves from the trees, we gather with new purpose.

In each other's company we find warmth against the approach of winter's cold.

We look to the bounty of harvest to sustain us while the earth sleeps.

We attend again to the wider circles of relationship, reminded of the connections on which we depend.

In each face at the table—some softening with age, some blooming into maturity—we see the human story revealed, the journey we each walk from mystery to mystery.

In the touch of each hand there is cause for gratitude: for our lives, for the love we share, even if imperfect and not always fully realized, love that each deserves, of which each is capable; love that every day of our journeys we are given new opportunities to accept and to give.

GOD, AGAIN
February 2, 2014

READINGS

Self Portrait by David Whyte

It doesn't interest me if there is one God or many gods.
I want to know if you belong or feel abandoned.
If you know despair or can see it in others.
I want to know
  if you are prepared to live in the world
  with its harsh need to change you.
If you can look back with firm eyes
  saying this is where I stand.
I want to know if you know
  how to melt into that fierce heat of living
  falling toward the center of your longing.
I want to know if you are willing
  to live, day by day, with the consequence of love
  and the bitter unwanted passion of your sure defeat.

www.davidwhyte.com/english_self.html

Who is this who darkens counsel, speaking without
knowledge?
Where were you when I laid the earth's foundations?
Speak, if you have understanding.
Do you know who fixed its dimensions, or who
measured it with a line?
Onto what were its bases sunk?
Who set its cornerstone when the morning stars sang
together and all the divine beings shouted for joy? ...

Have you commanded the day to break, assigned the
dawn its place, so that it seizes the corners of the
earth and shakes the wicked out of it? ...

Have you penetrated to the sources of the sea, or
walked in the recesses of the deep?
Have the gates of death been disclosed to you?
Have you surveyed the expanses of the earth?
If you know of these—tell me.

Job 38:1-7; 12-13; 16-18

SERMON

The writer Eric Weiner tells of how one day he found
himself doubled over with abdominal pain in a New York City
emergency room. As he shivered in his paper gown waiting for
the doctor, a nurse arrived to draw some blood. The woman,
about his age with features and an accent that seemed to him
Caribbean or West African, paused and said quietly, "Have you
found your God yet?"

Taken aback, he stammered, "Why?" Did she know
something he didn't, he wondered. She didn't reply but just

gave him what seemed like a wise, knowing look and left.

Weiner's medical episode ended uneventfully—turns out to have been just a severe attack of gas—but the nurse's question weighed on him. Had he found his God ... yet? It set him wondering. She wasn't asking whether he had found a God or the God or just plain God, but his God, as it there were one out there for him, waiting.

For a while he put it aside. It wasn't a question he felt was relevant to his life. God, religion: he had left all that stuff behind in his youth, growing up in a culturally Jewish but not especially religious household. And besides he very much saw himself as a rationalist—someone who looks to science and reason as a guide to living—and he saw little about the notion of God that seemed rational to him.

Still, he wrote, he had to admit that in his experience, while "reason is an excellent tool for solving problems (it) offers little guidance in identifying which problems we should solve and why." In the words of G.K. Chesterton: reason doesn't account well for those moments in life that "bewilder the intellect, yet utterly quiet the heart."

There was something about that nurse's question that nagged at him, but he had no notion of how to begin to answer it. Searching for a spiritual category where he might plant his flag, he gave up, declaring himself simply a "confusionist" armed with this credo: "We have absolutely no idea what our religious views are. We're not even sure we have any, but we're open to the unexpected, and believe—no, hope—there is more to life than meets the eye."

For Weiner, this puzzlement was the goad for a journey that he recounted in a best-selling book *Man Seeks God*. The book tells of Weiner's travels around the world to learn about and experience eight religious traditions, ranging from Sufism and Buddhism to Franciscan Catholicism and Kabbalah.

Few of us have the resources for such an adventure, but for many of us Weiner's label of "confusionist" rings a bell, especially when it comes to this notion of God.

I remember when I was around nine or ten years old playing with a friend by a stream near my home when he casually asked me, "Do you believe in God?" I didn't know what to say, but to hide my embarrassment I just mumbled something like, I did, and that ended the conversation.

So, I guess I could date my own history of wrestling with the notion of God from that moment. It wasn't as if I had never heard of God. In my Unitarian Universalist religious education classes I had encountered God and gods from many cultures in many guises. But I had never been instructed on an answer to that bald question: Do you believe in God?

I know now that the stories I heard and the lessons participated in were intended not to deliver received answers on the mind-boggling questions that religion poses—who am I, what matters, where did I and all of this come from—but to encourage my wondering mind to work through them and come to answers that made sense to me, answers that surely would change as I changed and grew, but that were rooted in my own understanding and experience.

That has been true of this religion since the days of its founding in the early 19th century when William Ellery Channing declared that "the great end in religious instruction is not to stamp our minds upon the young, but to stir up their own; not to make them see with our eyes, but to look inquiringly and steadily with their own."

And it remains true of us today. When a volunteer teacher in our Spirit Play classes reads a story, he or she will invite the children to comment on it with a reflection that begins with the words, "I wonder..." I wonder how that felt, I wonder what they meant, I wonder why she said that. And you'll recognize that I'm inviting you as our worship theme for the month to do some wondering of your own.

Looking back on my childhood encounter, though, I see that there was something more than puzzlement behind my confused answer at the streamside: something that I now recognize as shame. Young as I was, I had lived long enough to perceive that at the time in the larger culture there was really only one socially acceptable answer to my friend's question, and I gave it.

Things have loosened a bit since the early 1960s, but the presumption is still strong, especially here in the South, that when asked, one will respond as I did. So, if nothing else it challenges people like us who find integrity affirming a range of responses, from "yes" to "no" to "Well, tell me what you mean by God," to broaden the conversation and work to find some clarity for ourselves.

Karen Armstrong begins her book *The Case for God* by declaring, "We are talking far too much about God these days, and what we say is often facile." God, she says, is bandied about by so many people in so many settings that we are left with the presumption that the concept of God should be easy. You know, God: Supreme Being, creator of all Things, infinitely loving, ultimately inscrutable, utterly transcendent, and yet counting every fallen sparrow. Simple!

Wait a minute: did you say simple? With so many imponderables wrapped around it, this tiny word quickly expands beyond our common capacity to make sense of it, and so it becomes a convenient screen on which we humans can project our hopes and fears; our aspirations and ambitions, pinning on attributes, such as pronouns—him, mostly; and motives—smiting these people, blessing those others.

Probably no work offers a more effective caution against this practice than the ancient Book of Job that I quoted earlier. You'll recall that the book begins with God looking down from on high and praising his good servant Job, while Satan insists the Job is only good because he's treated well. Test him, Satan says, and you'll see him curse you.

So, God does, inflicting him with every measure of disease and misfortune. But Job insists that he holds to his faith. Friends arrive, and while they commiserate, they suggest that Job must have done something to deserve all these ills, for God only punishes those who deserve it. This goes on for some time, and Job bemoans his outcast state until the figure of God breaks in with a long soliloquy, part of which you heard.

It is an amazing passage. As the writer Barbara Brown Taylor puts it, God speaks, not, apparently, because Job has been irresistibly persuasive in arguing why he has been ill-served, but, she says, "because God cannot stand one more minute of his yammering."

The language in these questions is lyrical—"Where were you when the morning stars sang together? Have you seen the gates of deep darkness?" I can imagine the writers pushing their imaginations to the limit—how to express the inconceivable? how to communicate how infinitely unknowable the ways of the universe are? The question that the book seems set up to answer—why do bad things happen to good people—is blown out of the water, and along with it the neat image of a friendly God who watches over us and finds us parking spots.

Forget that! The wisdom that Job offers us is that suffering happens, and we are left to make of our lives what we can. But, God? Well, back to the drawing board.

Karen Armstrong observes that theology, literally the study

of God, "is a very wordy discipline." People, she says, "have written reams and talked unstoppably about God." (Speaking from the experience of four years of seminary and ten years of ministry, I can only say, "Oh, preach it, Sister.") And while much of it is impenetrable and some of it is actually beautiful, it doesn't necessarily take us much closer to making sense of God, if there is any sense to be made.

Armstrong argues that the trouble began when in our modern age, the Christian church and its scholars took to applying the language of science—which she describes as "logos"—to the study of religion, which she says had been the imaginative realm of what she calls "mythos."

One unfortunate result of all this, she says, is that it pulled religion out of where it originated, as a rich and metaphorical guide to living, and set it up in the academy as an artifact for arcane study. The old image of scholars counting how many angels can dance on a pin was the product of this way of thinking.

In fact, Karen Armstrong argues, religion holds the most promise not as a place of proof texts, but as "a practical discipline that teaches us to discover new capacities of mind and heart." The notion of God, too, she says, works better when it comes out of the clouds, loses its pronouns and invites us to reflect on what is most deeply real and impinges on us most profoundly.

My colleague Galen Guengerich has argued for describing God as, in his words, "an experience that intimately and extensively connects me to all that is." And a consequence of this experience, he says, is to invite us to see ourselves as agents of the best there is, call it the divine, call it all that upholds life and love in the universe.

Could that be "your" God? Perhaps, perhaps not. The sense

of transcendence that Galen describes is something that all of us experience in one form or another, but there are many ways of framing it that need have nothing to do with God.

Our music today offers a sense of the variety of ways that transcendent appears to us. Joan Osbourne invites us to find the holy in the scrubby stranger on the bus, the "other" we avert our eyes to avoid. Pete Seeger believed he found all he ever needed in the songs he used to break through the boundaries that keep us human beings apart. And Mendelsohn's beautiful chorus lifts us up with its bounteous imagery of God as the unsleeping source of compassion that quickens our languishing hearts.

So, in answer to Eric Weiner's nurse, must we expect that at some time we will hitch our own spiritual wagon to some understanding of God? No, not necessarily, and really that's not the central question. I think that David Whyte's poem, which Bob read earlier, comes closer to the point. Called "Self Portrait," it is, I'm told, something he wrote one night in a period of spiritual crisis while he was looking in the mirror. So the person to whom he is speaking is one he knows well.

When you let go of the labels, the clever scripts that you've cobbled together for when the "religion" question comes up, when you are fully present to yourself: what do you see? To what, to whom do you belong? What is your answer when despair visits you? As the world pushes and prods, wheedles and pleads, how do you find your center?

Are you prepared to give yourself fully to the truth that lives within you? I love the vividness of his imagery—do you know how to melt, holding nothing back, into that fierce heat of living that feels like nothing less than falling toward the center of your longing?

And how will you live day by day with the consequences of all the commitments you have made in your life, the love that both nourishes and tears at your heart, knowing that one day all of it—you and I, too—will be gone?

Oh friends, let us set to wondering. Let us be good company, and let the space we create and hold here be the crucible for our work.

It matters not if there is one God or many Gods or any Gods, when it comes down to it. What matters is that we be witnesses to the beauty and wonder of the world, that we live with integrity and compassion, that we honor that ineffable transcendence in which we and all things participate, the stream that, as Tagore put its, runs through the world, that shouts in joy through the grasses and is rocked in the ocean cradle of birth and death, moving through us this very moment.

Meditation
April 2013

Who do we say that we are—
We fallible, gullible, quizzical sorts.
The question posed of a different person
in a different context
in a different time
circles back on us.

What would we take as a meaningful reply?
Would we tell of our history?
Would we calculate our physiognomy?
Would we take testimony of friends and relations?

  Or, would we tell of what first flickers in our minds
  at waking,
Or what echoes as slumber gathers us?
Would we name what we shrink from in fear,
Or what lights us up with beatific joy?
Or would we casually relate the surprise of a bird song
  that interrupted our reverie, a flash of color, and
  then gone?

UNTO THE SEVENTH GENERATION
June 16, 2013

Our story begins some five hundred years ago at a time of terrible feuds among people who have come to be known as the Iroquois in the region we now call upper New York state. The feuds had their origin in a long-standing practice called "mourning wars" that had entered a particularly bitter and bloody phase.

The practice was grounded in a belief about how the world worked. The people felt that there was a spiritual power that animated all things and that any time someone died the collective power of his or her family or clan was diminished. So, afterward, the family or tribe would hold a ceremony in which social role and duties would be transferred to someone else.

Of course, sometimes there was no one else to take that role, and there was much grieving. In time, however, if the grief did not abate, women of the household could demand that a war party be assembled to raid a neighboring tribe and seek captives to make up for the loss. In some cases, those captives would be integrated or even enslaved by the clan, but in others, if the grief were particularly severe, they could be ritually killed and cannibalized. During this particular period, this exchange of mourning wars was incessant with clans raiding each other, tit for tat, while the killing just went on and on.

Among these folks, was one man, Hiawatha—not Longfellow's noble savage but a very different figure—who had lost several daughters to this carnage and was driven mad by anger and depression.

In despair, he wandered off into the forest where he is said to have encountered what is described as a spiritual being who called himself Deganawidah, or the Peacemaker. The Peacemaker gave Hiawatha strings of shell beads and spoke words of condolence that dried his eyes, that opened his ears, that unstopped his throat and so on until his grief was removed and his reason was restored. Those acts were woven into a ritual that became the center of a new teaching that, the Peacemaker assured Hiawatha, would make wars of mourning unnecessary.

Hiawatha and the Peacemaker then traveled to surrounding tribes and in time persuaded them to join what was then called the Great League of Peace and Power. It was to be an alliance that would marshal the spiritual energy of every family group.

The five and, later, six Indian nations joined in this league became known as the Haudenosaunee, or people of the long house. The title refers to the large dwellings where the people lived, housing as many as twenty families, as well as the ethic they lived by, one that envisioned all members gathered around a common fire, respecting each other, involved in each other.

To secure and maintain the peace they declared, the League created a Grand Council made up of fifty leaders, or sachems, whose sole purpose was to prevent what was called "the disuniting of minds." As one observer put it, their notion of peace "did not imply a negotiated agreement backed by sanctions of international law and mutual interest, it was a matter of 'good thoughts' between nations, a feeling as much as a reality."

The council's purpose, then, was not to adopt laws—in fact, it had little power over individual tribes—but to cultivate and deepen relationship. The League ended the mourning wars, but honored the spirit behind them by granting the leading women of each tribe the right to select each sachem.

It was among the sachems or chiefs in these councils that the notion that one should act with an eye to the welfare of the seventh generation ahead was articulated. In a forum focused on relationship, not only with each other but also with the land on which they depended, full of ceremonies of thanksgiving and honor for each other, such a declaration was a natural outcome.

Today, it is curious now to see what a popular meme that phrase has become in our culture. Run "Seventh Generation" through Google and your first hit is a company that has trademarked it for their line of home cleaning products, followed soon after by another selling disposable diapers.

And why not? You could argue that the popularity of the phrase among marketers is a testament to how powerful the idea behind it is, even if we seem to miss the irony of finding that label on a package of paper towels. But before I get too high and mighty, let me make a confession—I have bought those paper towels; I have bought those diapers. Because, even if there are hardly more conspicuous examples of products that contradict the ethic of environmental sustainability, that contribute to this nation's ballooning waste stream and the depredation of its forests and water courses, even so there are times when paper towels come in handy—not often, of course, I usually use cloth—and, well, are cloth diapers really so much better than disposable? And, gosh, looking at the labels of these products they seem more "environmentally-friendly"—boy, talk about a loaded term—than others. I mean, don't they say they're made from more recycled or recyclable materials?

And ... and ... and ... Well, you get the picture. This is where we live, isn't it? There's hardly a soul today who doesn't at least give a nod to the environment in how she or he goes about their lives, and hardly a soul who feels that he or she is doing enough.

And yet, however we feel, the fact remains that the world is changing before our eyes. We see it in birds or perennials appearing earlier in spring, in pests once killed by winter freezes sticking around, in colossal storms spawning killer tornados and hurricanes. Our climate is clearly in play, but we have no way of knowing how it will play out.

Just a month ago, scientists reported that the average level of carbon dioxide in the air has reached 400 parts per million, the highest it's been for 3 million years, a time before humans had evolved as a species. What does that mean? Well, because carbon dioxide traps heat in the atmosphere that would otherwise escape into space, it likely will lead to overall warming of the earth.

But of course our climate is complex, the result of the interplay of many forces that we are only beginning to understand. So, the effects vary from place to place, and sometimes in unexpected ways: in one place a killing drought, in another, monsoon-like storms; in some places spring-like winters, in others increased snowfall. But the overall trend has been warmer. Overall global temperatures are higher than at any time in the past 4,000 years; last year, 2012, was the hottest on record in the U.S. And the effects are obvious: mountain glaciers and polar icecaps are shrinking; sea levels are rising. And around the world these rising temperatures are either stressing or killing forests and coral reefs, and changing the habitats for creatures ranging from insects to antelope, extinguishing some and threatening others.

The fossil record says that the last time the concentration of carbon dioxide was 400 parts per million, average temperatures were four to seven degrees warmer and sea levels were much higher. We can't be sure of how things will go now, though, since it takes time for the effects of warming to ripple through the Earth's systems.

And, of course, we have every reason to believe that carbon dioxide levels will continue to rise. That's because we have a pretty good idea as to why they're rising. We've endured the debates as to the causes over the last half century, and at this point it's all over but the shouting. We humans are the drivers on this bus. Some two centuries of industrial development have disrupted this planet so profoundly that we have put our own survival and that of many of our fellow creatures in peril.

It's astonishing to think that we comparatively tiny beings, so easily tossed by storm and tide, could make such an impact on this vast globe. Yet it turns out that the conditions that sustain beings like us are fairly narrow, and it doesn't take all that much to knock them off kilter. We need only look at the record of history to find civilizations that have disappeared due to fairly minor shifts in weather. What can we look forward to in a world warmer than humankind has ever known?

It's a scary prospect, so it's little wonder that so many of us choose simply to avert our eyes, or satisfy ourselves as doing our part by buying "green" and recycling our trash. Part of what makes this so hard is that the problem is woven into the details of our lives as we now live them. Every time we drive our cars, or ride in a plane, every light or appliance we switch on, plug in, or boot up adds carbon dioxide to the air.

It makes me understand a dimension of Hiawatha's grief of

half a millennium ago. Here we sit in the 21st century with that which sustains life on this planet under assault from the very patterns and practices of our living, and not just any practices, but those that we have come to equate with "the good life," the life we aspire to.

What a disconnect! What an impossible irony! But it's not lost, I believe, on our psyches. It may offer one explanation for the dystopic images scattered across our films and video games of a ravaged world with Hiawatha-like figures wandering the landscape in frustration and despair.

But the story of the Iroquois offers us more the just an image of despair. It also offers a frame for hope. The figure who appears to Hiawatha, linked closely in the story to one of the creator figures in that people's mythology, finds a way to release him from his grief: in the story, to dry his weeping eyes, to open his ears, to unstop his throat so that his sorrow may be relieved and his reason restored.

Climate changed has been framed as a technical problem in need of technical fixes, and yet, to be honest, like the grieving Hiawatha, I'm not sure we are yet in the place where we are ready to sort this out in a rational way. About a decade ago, an engineering professor, Robert Socolow, detailed more than a dozen strategies, stabilizing wedges he called them, that he argued could slow and even halt the warming of the atmosphere.

They were things like dramatically expanding the use of photovoltaic cells to generate electricity, adding more nuclear power plants, even capturing and storing carbon. The problem was that every wedge required a monumental effort. In the case of photovoltaics, for example, to make any significant difference we would need arrays covering a surface of five million acres— about the size of Connecticut.

The question is not what we *can* do to solve this problem;

it's what we are prepared to do. In an interview at the time, Scolow said the task before us is on the scale of abolishing slavery. "It's the kind of issue," he said, "where something looked extremely difficult, and not worth it, and then people changed their minds."

Years ago as a science writer I got to cover the spring "booming" or mating rituals of prairie chickens in central Wisconsin. These endangered creatures surely would have been erased from that landscape long before I arrived but for the work of the naturalist Aldo Leopold. Leopold was most famous for arguing for the awakening of what he called "a land ethic": a way of looking at the world that, in his words, "enlarges the boundaries of community to include soils, waters, plants, and animals, or, collectively, the land."

These words echo those of the Peacemaker in the Iroquois story who invites Hiawatha to understand his identity more broadly and to see the larger spiritual unity of all things. When we in this religious tradition agree among ourselves to affirm and promote respect for the interdependent web of all existence of which we are a part, we make a similar connection.

Taking our lead from what the Iroquois discovered in their Grand Councils, while scientists strategize possible solutions to our approaching peril, the rest of us must be about the work of building of relationship. Remember that the Iroquois commitment to the "seventh generation" was rooted in their love for the people and the land of their present day.

And so it will be for us if we are to find a solution to the train wreck that climate change presents us. As Wendell Berry put it, love is not an abstract proposition. It is tied, in his words, to "particular things, places, people and creatures."

I can profess my love for the world and all things in it, but that alone has little purchase. When I can name what I love and tell how that love has changed my behavior, changed my thinking, changed my life, I am getting a little closer to the true thing. Again, from Wendell Berry, "Love proposes no abstract vision but the work of settled households and communities," communities that act, that take stands, that take risks, and still stay in relationship.

So, what is our work, as a settled community affirming respect for the interdependent web of all existence of which we are a part? It is a question I want to invite you to join me in answering. How might we as a people of memory and hope learn to widen our hearts to embrace a world now under assault by the very patterns and practices of our lives?

You have my commitment in the coming year to finding ways for us to engage in that conversation. We have long passed the time when we could delegate this issue to others. It is ours to confront, and it will require educating ourselves and thinking, and adjusting our lives to an emerging reality.

But, as Lew Patrie suggested earlier, it will also require deeper work fitting of a religious community. It will require learning to transcend the fear, despair and forgetfulness that paralyze us, that set us against each other, so that we might awaken to the wonder of our lives and each other, to the gift of a planet that seven times seven generations ahead might yet sustain our own kind and the vast web of life.

Meditation
September 2010

Listen to all that is present here today:
The pulse of heartbeat upon heartbeat,
pounding with fierce urgency,
breaking the wave crest of each dawning moment;
the sound of breath upon breath,
sweet air admitted into the chambers of our deep
bellows
to the point of satisfying fullness,
then expelled back into the world,
preparing us, once again, to receive.
These rhythms carry us
along what is sometimes the gentle stream,
sometimes the wild flume ride of our lives.
And they offer us a bridge to the lives of our fellows,
beings both fragile and strong,
confused and confident,
lacking and fulfilled: in short, like us.
And so we listen:
Behind the strident voice, the hesitant question,
the polished argument, the silent glance
is a beating heart and suspiring lungs,
preparing, once again, to receive.

CLOSING WORDS

The preacher closes the worship service with a "benediction," good words intended to send the congregation on its way lifted up, ready for a week ahead of the challenges that life presents us until we meet again. And that draws attention to one of the peculiarities of this trade. While the worship service is framed in a moment of time, the sermon is never quite finished. It is the people who experience it who complete it, who weigh what there is within it that may have relevance for their lives and what they will do with it. It becomes part of an ongoing conversation that is shaped by our lives together.

In a sense this book is a record of one end of that conversation in a snapshot of time. I wonder what a record of the other end of that conversation would look like. In any event, I am grateful to have had this conversation and that the conversation continues. And in the end my hope is that it these words have any effect it will be to have been of service to the great work of liberal religion, the freeing of hearts and minds to see the unity in which we all live with common dreams in a common destiny.

To order by mail or online please contact:

Pisgah Press
PO Box 1427   Candler, NC 28715
pisgahpress@gmail.com
828-301-8968

www.ingramcontent.com/pod-product-compliance
Lightning Source LLC
Chambersburg PA
CBHW060758050426
42449CB00008B/1446